THE ART OF WRITING A RESUME

Sajitha Jayaprakash

First Edition : 2010

Himalaya Publishing House

MUMBAI • NEW DELHI • NAGPUR • BENGALURU • HYDERABAD • CHENNAI • PUNE • LUCKNOW • AHMEDABAD • ERNAKULAM • BHUBANESWAR • INDORE • KOLKATA

First Edition : 2010

Published by : Mrs. Meena Pandey for **Himalaya Publishing House Pvt. Ltd.,**
"Ramdoot", Dr. Bhalerao Marg, Girgaon, **Mumbai - 400 004.**
Phone: 2386 01 70/2386 38 63, Fax: 022-2387 71 78
Email: himpub@vsnl.com Website: www.himpub.com

Branch Offices

New Delhi : "Pooja Apartments", 4-B, Murari Lal Street, Ansari Road, Darya Ganj, **New Delhi - 110 002.** Phone:23270392, 23278631 Fax: 011-23256286

Nagpur : Kundanlal Chandak Industrial Estate, Ghat Road, **Nagpur - 440 018.** Phone: 2738731, 3296733 Telefax : 0712-2721215

Bengaluru : No. 16/1 (Old 12/1), 1st Floor, Next to Hotel Highlands, Madhava Nagar, Race Course Road, **Bengaluru - 560 001.** Phone : 22281541, 22385461, Telefax: 080-22286611

Hyderabad : No. 3-4-184, Lingampally, Besides Raghavendra Swamy Matham,Kachiguda, **Hyderabad - 500 027.** Phone: 040-27560041, 27550139, Mobile:- 09848130433

Chennai : No. 85/50, Bazullah Road, T. Nagar, **Chennai - 600 017.** Phone: 044-28144004/28144005

Pune : First Floor, "Laksha" Apartment, No. 527, Mehunpura, Shaniwarpeth (Near Prabhat Theatre), **Pune - 411 030.** Phone: 020-24496323/24496333

Lucknow : C-43, Sector - C, Ali Gunj, **Lucknow - 226 024.** Phone: 0522-2339329

Ahmedabad : 114, "SHAIL", 1st Floor, Opp. Madhu Sudan House, C.G.Road, Navrang Pura, **Ahmedabad– 380 009.** Phone: 079-26560126, Mobiles:- 09327324149,09314679413

Ernakulam : 39/104 A, Lakshmi Apartment, Karikkamuri Cross Rd., Ernakulam, **Cochin – 622011**, Kerala. Phone: 0484-2378012, 2378016, Mob.: 09344199799

Bhubaneswar: 5 Station Square, **Bhubaneswar (Orissa) - 751 001.** Mobile:- 9861046007

Indore : Kesardeep Avenue Extension, 73, Narayan Bagh, Flat No. 302, IIIrd Floor, Near Humpty Dumpty School, Narayan Bagh, **Indore 452 007(M.P.),** Mobile:- 09301386468

Kolkata : 108/4, Beliaghata Main Road, Near ID Hospital, Opp. SBI Bank, **Kolkata** - 700 010, Mobile :- 09910440956

DTP by : HPH, Editorial Office, Bhandup (Sunanda)

Printed by : Esquire Press, Mumbai

Dedicated to:

My sister, Deepa (Deepu),
my brother-in-law, Krishna Kumar,
and my only nephew, Arjun (Ananthu).

ABOUT THE BOOK

A resume is document dedicated to you because it is about you. It is a brief sketch of your goals, background and achievements. It serves as an introduction or first impression of your qualifications to an employer. Hence, it is probably one of the most important documents that you will ever compose. It is designed to sell you as it is used to showcase your special talents and reflect your uniqueness to potential employers. Keep in mind though that resumes are usually used for 20-30 seconds. Hence you should take time and effort to format it such a way that a person should be able to locate the information quickly.

I have been involved in the interviewing and the recruiting process for about nine years. Over the years I have realized that though we have changed the job search process drastically over the last decade, we still follow certain old rules as far as creating resumes are concerned.

Now, we search for job on the intranet and actively use e-mails to send resumes. Since the medium of job search and applying for jobs have changed, the rules for creating resumes should also change, by taking certain factors into consideration.

There are many perceptions about writing resumes. Though there is no dearth of books on this subject, there is definitely a lack of good reference books written by people with industry experience—those who actually review the resumes, conduct interviews, and select candidates. After interviewing and recruiting candidates for many years, I have come to recognize quickly what impresses me and what does not, what makes me consider a candidate, what makes me call a candidate for an interview, and what immediately closes the door on the candidates. The information presented here is based on my *experiences with resumes.*

This book is different because it is the result of practical experience. Moreover, it does not directly start telling you how to create a workable resume.

Instead, it will tell you:

- The purpose of the resume.
- What it is and what it is not?
- The commonly made errors while creating resumes.
- The myths and the misconceptions associated with the resumes.
- Some tips on creating usable, focused, and impressive resumes.
- How to create an impressive resume?
- The importance of using action words.

It will make you think out of the box and will help you make a well thought about decision before you start writing a resume. Once you understand the skills and characteristics that most employer seek, you can tailor your job search communication—your resume, cover letter, and interview language—to showcase how well your background aligns with their requirements.

Don't be scared about creating a resume, just follow the instructions provided in this book. I sincerely hope this book is of use to you. Good luck in your job search and wishing you all the best!

— ***Sajitha Jayaprakash***

CONTENTS

Chapter 1 Resume—What Is It?

The chapter will tell you and give you an overview of the resume, bio-data, curriculum vitae and explain the differences between them. It will also tell what a resume is, and most importantly, what it is not. This chapter contains the following topics:

- ❐ **Section 1.1:** What's the Right Word?
  - — **Section 1.1.1:** Resume
  - — **Section 1.1.2:** Curriculum Vitae
  - — **Section 1.1.3:** Bio-data
- ❐ **Section 1.2:** Purpose of a Resume
- ❐ **Section 1.3:** What It Is Not?
- ❐ **Section 1.4:** Think Without Any Limitation
- ❐ **Section 1.5:** Question Yourself

1.1 What's the Right Word?

Resume, bio-data, and curriculum vitae (or CV as it is more commonly known as) is often used interchangeably in India. Resume is an American term where as curriculum vitae is a term that is more acceptable in areas like New Zealand, some European countries (like Ireland, Britain, Scotland), and in some parts of Canada.

Is there any difference between the three? There surely is!

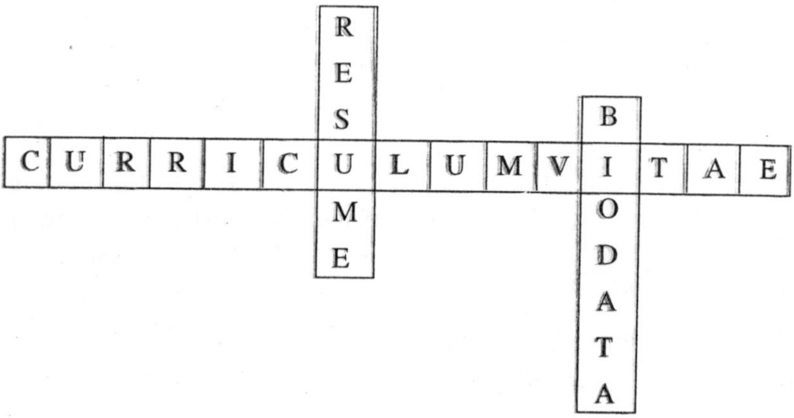

1.1.1 Resume

Resume is a brief summary (of two or three pages) of your qualifications, skills, work history, experiences, and accomplishment specific to the job being applied. It is designed to capture the interest of a prospective employer with the purpose of securing an interview.

Thus, the three main components of the resume are:

- Purpose (for details, see Section 1.2)
- Content (for details, see Chapter 5)
- Design (for details, see Chapter 4)

You can create several resume specific to different positions or different organizations, based on their requirements.

Resume	Curriculum Vitae
• Concise in its information, about 2 or 3 pages in length	• Not concise and can be more than pages 4-5 (or more) in length.
• Tailored to fit the requirement of the prospective company or employer	• Tailored to fit the requirement of the prospective company or employer.
• Limited with traditions categories/sections	• Not limited with traditions categories/sections.
• Used in corporate, industry, private, and public sectors.	• Used mainly in medical, education, and research institutions.
• May contain a job objective.	• Contains no objective statement
• Contains information that is only relevant to the position being applied.	• Each category is well-defined and is complete with well-detailed information (even if it is not relevant to the position being applied).

1.1.2 Curriculum Vitae

A curriculum vitae (CV) is used primarily when applying for international, academic, education, scientific or research positions. It is also used when applying for fellowships or grants. The primary differences between a resume and a curriculum vitae are:

- Length: How big/lengthy it is.
- Content: What is included in them.
- Purpose: What they are used for.

In addition to the basics, a CV should include research experience, publications, grants, fellowships, professional associations, awards, and other information which is relevant to the position you are applying for. As with a resume, you may not need different versions of a CV for different type of positions because it is not specific to the position you have applied for and contains all the details and information.

- List out and explain every detail of education, employment, achievements, and skills.

- Add all work experiences (previous or current) along with elaborated job descriptions.
- Include all training and seminars attended.
- Voluntary work and social affiliations if any.

This is the reason why curriculum vitae is usually used when applying for academic, medical, and scientific jobs because employers in these industries prefer to know all the details of each applicant thoroughly.

All these factors make a curriculum vitae more elaborate, descriptive, and longer than a resume. The Americans have now begun to accept curriculum vitae as longer form of resumes. Similarly, even the English have begun to accept resume as a shorter version of curriculum vitae. So, now we can safely say that while a resume is a brief summary of your education, skills and experiences, a curriculum vitae is a longer and more detailed document.

1.1.3 Bio-data

In some Asian communities like India, a bio-data is essentially the details of the person put together to be used for marriage-related purposes. The bio-data is exchanged with the parents, or the relatives of the prospective suitors. The purpose is similar to that of a resume—to eliminate some candidates from the pool of prospective suitors before meeting the prospective suitors.

The bio-data generally contains the information that is available in a resume, but apart from work history, salary information, and educational background, the emphasis is also on the following:

- The physical attributes, such as age, date of birth, height, weight, hair/skin/eye colour.
- Details about the family—father, mother, and siblings.
- The educational background, career related information, and other details of the parents and siblings.

1.2 Purpose of a Resume

The sole purpose of the resume is to win an interview. It is a professional introduction and an advertisement of your skills, expertise, and knowledge.

For each position that you apply for, you may assume that there is an average of 500 applicants. So, you have to make it easy for the hiring manager to make a choice between you and the other candidates. The only way to achieve that is by writing a noticeable resume.

A well-written resume will not get you the job, but it will get you an opportunity of an interview, which may eventually lead to a job offer. A well-written and well-presented resume improves your chances of being noticed and interviewed. If it makes the interviewer notice you, sets you ahead of the competition, and helps you secure an interview, then it has given you a distinct advantage, and will go beyond its purpose of just securing you an interview. So, it is true to say that a resume is a stepping stone to getting a job.

The first job is usually difficult to get and that makes resume a very important factor in helping you securing an interview. The resume should be appropriate to the requirement of the job, highlighting appropriate skills, qualities, and experience (if any).

Instead of following a bunch of rules/tips blindly, you have to use them to your advantage by choosing what is right for you. The purpose and design of the resume can up to an extent, depend on your personal choice, but keep it neat, simple, and professional.

With a little extra effort, you can create a resume that can stir the interest of the prospective employers and make you stand out as a superior candidate for the job you are seeking. Even if you face fierce competition with people more qualified, experienced, and/or skilfull than you, it will give you an opportunity to be invited for the interview.

After that, it is up to you to perform and convince the interviewers that you are the person for the job.

1.3 What It Is Not?

Many people think resume to be a detailed career history which is a colossal mistake. A resume should not be:

- **An autobiography:** Unfortunately, most of the times the resumes received by the employers are personal job history essays running into four or five pages, containing unnecessary and irrelevant information. The information may be true and of value to you, but not to the interviewers.

  It is true that most of the content of a resume is focused on the job history, experience, and the skills, but it should be written with the intention of creating interest and arousing curiosity in the minds of people reading the resume. It must persuade the employer to call you for an interview.

- **Written for the heck of it:** Some people write a resume with the idea of getting the task done, without any passion and/or interest. This lack of interest reflects on the resume. If you are not interested in creating a resume, don't do it! Wait till you are able to concentrate on the job.

- **Written for self-satisfaction:** Some people write a resume because they have to write one to apply for the job. They create a resume that seems right and perfect to them. They really don't care about the content and format.

- **Written with the focus of getting the job:** Do not create a resume containing all the details with the objective of getting you a job. Create it to obtain an interview. When reading your resume, the prospective employer or the hiring manager should generate enough interest in you to contact and invite you for an interview.

  If you are called for an interview, you can perform well, answer to their satisfaction, and attempt to get the job. Use the interview to provide a more detailed explanation of your accomplishments mentioned in the resume.

Strive to be clear and concise which also ensures that the resume does not run into pages. You need to realize that a resume can be your ticket for getting your dream job. So don't create a format driven, senseless, boring history about your work!

1.4 Think Without Any Limitation

To write an effective resume, you have to learn the art of powerful writing. To create a good resume, you will have to answer four questions:

1. What is the purpose of your resume? [*purpose*]
2. What kind of information you need to add to the resume? [*content*]
3. What are the requirements and the expectations of the employer? [*specific content*]
4. What is the best way to write the resume so that the prospective employer can easily locate the information they are looking for? [*design and layout*]

If you can answer these questions, you will get a good idea of the information you have to add and what not to add in your resume. Once you have a draft in place, you can think with a new perspective:

1. See some new connections between your work experiences.
   - What you want to do.
   - The skills you have.
   - What the employer is looking for.
2. List your qualities, abilities, and skills you think would be most important to the recruiter doing the hiring.
3. Try to cover all possible aspects by thinking globally.

1.5 Question Yourself

If you do not address the requirements of the employer, they will not respond to your resume. Ask yourself a few question (and answer them as well):

- What does the employer want? [*need analysis*]
  - — Do you have the skill set that is required for the job? [*skill set*]
  - — Do you have valid experience they are looking for? [*experience*]
  - — Do you have the required knowledge? [*knowledge*]
- What abilities and skills do you need for that position? [*skill analysis*]
- What would make you the perfect candidate for the job? [*self-analysis*]
  - — Does the company and their product line interest you? [*product interest*]
  - — Do you want to be a part of the team? [*profile*]
  - — Do you have any skills/talents you have not used, but can use in the job? [*skills*]
- What sets you apart from an exceptionally good candidate? [*mutual analysis*]

I am sure most of your wish you could read the minds of the employers and understand what they are actually looking to understand the unique combination of skills and values they seek.

Many of you would also like to unlock the secret formula to winning the hearts of the employers. Don't worry. The good news is that once you understand the skills and characteristics that most employer seek, you can tailor your resume, cover letter, and interview to showcase how well your background aligns with the requirements of the employer.

1.5.1 Fresher

Apart from the common skills and personal values, the recruiters look for some specific traits in the freshers. They would look for a good blend of personal traits, job-related skills, and/or certification. They also look for the following aspects:

- Is the resume tailor-made for the position applied?
- Is the resume sent specifically for the advertised position or to a number of job sites or other organizations?
- Is the education relevant to the position?
- Does the skills qualify for the position?
- Does the resume cover all the job requirements mentioned in the advertisement?
- Is the resume neat and to the point?
- Is the resume short and concise, yet complete?
- Does the applicant appear to be over qualified? Is there any brief, but valid explanation why the person has applied for the job?
- Is the education related information listed in reverse chronological order (masters degree, graduation, twelfth (HSC), tenth (SSC), etc.)?
- Does the information include only what would interest you.
- Has the person used strategic choices to organize, order, and convey the skills sets and other information.
- Does the resume highlight irrelevant skills?

Example: *When the position requires engineering skills, does it also stress on management skills.*

1.5.2 Experienced Candidate

The recruiters may look for some more additional aspects in an experienced candidate than what they would look for in candidates without experience:

- Is the applicant a job hopper?
- Does the resume highlight irrelevant skills and responsibilities?
- Is the work experience listed in reverse chronological order?
- Does the resume include advanced training that shows that the applicant has emphasized on enriching and updating his/her experience with additional classes, seminars, workshops or conferences?
- Are there any gaps in the job history that are unexplained?
- Does the resume demonstrate that the applicant is a self-starter or shows initiative?
- Are the experience, skill sets, and education of the applicant required for this job?
- Is the format of the resume consistent?
- Are there omitted dates, descriptions, references, etc., for some positions but not for others?
- Is the information genuine or does it appear to be padded or fudged?

Chapter 2 Myths and Misconceptions

This chapter discusses the following myths and the related truths about job-hunting and resume writing which will help in making your job search successful and less stressful:

- **Myth 1:** Advertisements Represent the Jobs Available
- **Myth 2:** Register at Several Job Sites to Get Many Interviews
- **Myth 3:** Decrease/Increase Your Salary Demands
- **Myth 4:** Don't Promote Yourselves
- **Myth 5:** The Most Qualified Candidate Will Get the Job
- **Myth 6:** Cover Letters Are Not Important
- **Myth 7:** Lengthier the Resume, The Better
- **Myth 8:** Higher Education Improves the Value of the Resume
- **Myth 9:** Experience Improves the Value of the Resume
- **Myth 10:** It is OK to Make Some Changes in the Resume

Myth 1: Advertisements Represent the Jobs Available

At the most, only about 15-20% of all available jobs are publicly advertised in mediums like newspaper and online job sites. The higher the position and salary, the less likely the position will be advertised in such medium. The vast majority of the job openings are part of the hidden job market. How can job-seekers discover these jobs?

- Most of such jobs are advertised on the related online forums. The reason being that only people with interest and experience will be members of such forums. Hence, a whole lot of unsuitable and uninterested candidates are already filtered out.
- Networking is another effective job search tool you can use. Networking is about building relationships with people who can help you in your job search. It does not mean that you need to ask everyone you know if they have a job for you.

Myth 2: Register at Several Job Sites to Get Many Interviews

This is one of the most prevalent misconceptions in job-hunting process amongst the youngsters. They feel that once they have applied online, they will receive dozens of interview calls. Wrong! Registering with job sites is an option that might get you plenty of information about the available jobs. It does not necessarily guarantee you an interview or a job. Ideally only one or two of the 20-30 odd e-mails you may receive from the recruiters who refer to your resume in the job sites will be of any remote use to you.

This kind of job-search be useful to you only if you are applying to specific positions for which you are perfectly qualified. You must be proactive in your job search and you must follow-up every job lead. You may not be qualified for that specific position, but the employer may have other openings that hasn't been advertised or they may know of other futuristic openings.

Myth 3: Decrease/Increase Your Salary Demands

Decreasing or increasing your salary demands will not make you an attractive or eligible candidate for the job. Your salary demands should be within acceptable range for the job you are seeking. It should also be within the range of industry, job profile, and location of the employer. Increasing or decreasing the salary demand will not make you an attractive candidate.

- If you are good at your job (first do a reality check), you should never lower your salary demands because:
  - It will make you appear desperate for the job.
  - The recruiters will start feeling vary about your experience and skills and chances are you will not be considered for the job offer however suitable you may be.
  - Even if you get the job, you would most likely not be happy at work when you see colleagues with lesser experience and skills earning more than you.

  On the other hand, if you are really desperate for a job, say after a lay-off or if you are without a job after a long time, you may lower your salary expectations.

- You should never increase your salary demands unnecessarily specially if you are not qualified in terms of skills and experience for the job. Doing so will only make you appear unreasonable and an expensive candidate. Even if you get the job, you will be looked upon as an underperformer.
- Many of you may go by market value. I have come across many candidates who give reasons like, *"The running market rate for a fresher for ABCD position is Rs. XYZ/-. So, I expect the same."*

  Though it is good to know the market value and rate, you should also know your own value and worth. The market value is for a certain level of skill sets and knowledge for certain level of expertise. If you don't have them, you don't fall into the market value criteria at all.

Employers prefer candidates who are well qualified for the job, have the necessary skills and experience, and come relatively inexpensive. But, it is also true that if the candidates have the right skills, attitude, and the interviewers collectively feel that they are really capable, they will be willing to pay as much or even more. As a rule, never be the first one to bring up the salary related topic. Let the employer raise the topic.

Myth 4: Don't Promote Yourselves

Job hunting is all about marketing yourself to the employers. It requires you to often use time and effort to highlight some key skills when creating your resumes to get an interview call.

You have to take effort to show the employer why you are the best person for the job. You need to make the employer believe that there is no one better than you. In today's job-hunting environment, the most successful candidates are those who apply the principles of marketing to themselves.

Creating a suitable resume is similar to the advertisements that the companies have used for years to successfully sell their products. Use the resume as an advertisement about you to promote yourself.

Myth 5: The Most Qualified Candidate Will Get the Job

One of the biggest misconception about interview or job search is that the most qualified or the most experienced candidate will get the job. It is true that the recruiters or the employers have some basic qualification in mind which they try to fulfill. But they are not necessarily interested in the most qualified candidate. They are interested in recruiting the right candidate.

Example: *If an organization recruits only engineers for a specific job function, they will shortlist the candidates based on that criteria. Candidates with B.Sc. or M.Sc. background will not be considered at all. This is because the basic educational qualification that is required for*

> *the job is an engineering degree.*
>
> *But after this shortlisting process, it is not necessary that the candidate with the highest percentage of marks or best experience be shortlisted for the interview or will get the job.*

You will get the interview based on your qualification, but you will get the job if the employer thinks there is a strong enough match of your skills, education, and experience to do the job. The candidate with the best mix of qualifications, skills, experience, attitude, and rapport with the interviewer(s) will get the job.

So, do not get too over confident if you are the most qualified person and do not get too discouraged if you have low percentage or lesser experience than that of others. You have to prove your worth during the interview and prove why you are the best person to fill the job.

Myth 6: Cover Letters Are Not Important

A cover letter is a letter of introduction and must be an integral part of your job search strategy. A very common feeling is that a cover letter is not important when you apply for the job. The truth is, you should send a cover letter written specifically for the position and company you are applying to.

- A cover letter written for the needs and requirements of a position for one organization will not be useful for a similar position in another organization. It should be specific to the skills and experience you are applying for.
- Cover letter for different positions in the same organization must also be different. It should be specific to the position you are applying for.

So, you need to carefully read the requirements of the job and create a cover letter that is specific to that particular position. If you cannot create a cover letter, ensure to add an objective in the resume so that the employer understands the skills you possess and the kind of job you are seeking. For details, see Chapter 7, Cover Letter.

Myth 7: Lengthier the Resume, the Better

Some candidates send resumes that look like thesis of their work profile running into pages containing worthless and repetitive information. The purpose of a resume is to market yourself. It should meet the needs of your reader. It should tell them why they should consider you for the given position.

- It should be visually pleasing and appealing to the readers.
- Avoid cluttered paragraphs where the readers have to wade through the text to try and figure out what they are supposed to read.
- In an attempt to create shorter resume, avoid unreadable, squashed, and small font size that makes the reader squint.
- The layout of your resume should be neat and professional. It should allow the reader access the information quickly.
- The information should be is easy to read. The reader should be able to scan your resume efficiently and effectively and easily locate the information they are looking for.
- Use action words whereever required.
- Make effective use of lists, bullets, and highlights.

For details, refer to Chapter 8, 25 Tips for Creating a Resume.

Myth 8: Higher Education Improves the Value of the Resume

The education section of a resume is the one most job seekers are obsessed with, specially if the candidate does not have the relevant experience. In some cases, unless and until there is an absolute necessity for a specific educational qualification, hiring decisions are made based on other skills of the candidate.

Some profession requires a specialized degree, (e.g., doctors, lawyers, CA, etc.).

Example: *For vacancy of a doctor you cannot take an experienced person with M.Sc. or Pharmaceutical background. You will recruit a person with an MBBS degree even if the person has no experience. It is because it is a matter of appropriate knowledge and also, it is a matter of life and death.*

But in IT industry, the recruiters can lax the experience and educational requirements if they find the right combination skills in a lesser experienced person. Though higher education is important, it is not the driving force behind hiring decisions.

Example: *An organization follows the policy of recruiting engineers with computer background for software testing positions. While shortlisting the resumes they find a candidate, Rajesh with M.Sc. Physics background who has done a course in software testing. After the telephonic talk, they find Ravi to be confident. He seems to have the potential and so invite him for a personal interview.*

Though he was pitted against engineers, Rajesh was confident and displayed certain soft skills that the interviewers were looking for. After a lot of deliberation, they decided to give Rajesh a chance to prove his worth, which he did.

Myth 9: Experience Improves the Value of the Resume

For some positions, experience is necessary, essential, and important, but other skills and factors are also taken into consideration when evaluating a candidate. Education, experience, skills, knowledge, and attitude are interwoven factors. The interviewers cannot consider them separately.

Interviewers take the final decision after taking into consideration all these aspects.

Example: *The job description reads: Seeking front desk executive with pleasing personality with experience in some administration related activities. Experienced candidate holding a degree from a reputed college may apply.*

Candidate 1: *Rose has worked as a front desk executive for 2 years. Before that, while doing her graduation, she worked part-time as a trainee administrative personal, because she had some personal problems. Since she got a full-time job as a front desk executive, she decided to discontinue her college education as there was financial constraints at home.*

Rose is hardworking, has a pleasing personality, with positive attitude, did not talk about the financial problems until the interviewers prompted to find out why she did not complete her education, though she received good marks and seemed to be a good student.

Candidate 2: *Sarita has a bachelors degree from a well known college. She has two years experience as a front desk executive. In fact she has been handling a complex multiline phone system.*

Sarita was confident, but a bit overconfident and little arrogant. She comes across as a pushy character.

Who would you hire, Rose or Sarita? Chances are that you named Rose as the clear winner because her experience and skills supercedes Sarita's education. Though Sarita has a degree and has worked with multiline phone system as the advertisement mentioned, Rose will be able to get into the job with little or no training. You will not have to spend—time, money, and resources to train her.

Myth 10: It is OK to Make Some Changes in the Resume

People are usually under the impression that if they lack the educational requirements or the experience described in the job description they won't be considered a serious candidate. So, they may feel compelled to stretch the truth in order to compete with their counterparts who may have more experience and the required skills.

You may often feel that a small tweak in the resume is harmless if it can get you an interview and later the job. But you may not be aware that this tweak in the resume can land you in serious trouble. You may not loose your job, but you will loose the credibility and people will assume you to be a dishonest person. For more information about fudging and doctoring the resumes, see Appendix A, Fudging Resumes.

Chapter 3

Errors While Creating Resumes

You will have to take care not to make some commonly made errors while creating a resume. In this chapter we discuss such errors.

When we think of creating a resume, the first question that comes in mind is, *"What's so great about it?"*

- Someone just out of college would think, *"I have passed with 85% of marks in all the subjects. So, my resume will stand out from the rest and I shall surely get an interview call."*
- An experienced person might think, *"I have worked with reputed companies and have an impressive record. I am sure to get the job."*

But is it not as easy as that? In reality, creating a resume is no easy task!

3.1 Having No Specific Goals

A resume without a target or a goal is like a map without identifying markers, which does not have any hope of a destination. Many people send in resumes stating, *"Please accept my candidature for any suitable position in your organization"*. If you believe that it is the responsibility of the hiring manager or potential employer to determine what role or position the person applying for the job will best fit in, you are mistaken.

These days, no one has the time nor the inclination to sort out such resumes and forward them to the appropriate department heads. The hiring managers are interested in hiring candidates who are focused, know about the job profile, and has keen interest in that area of work. They are not interested in hiring the confused souls.

"By recording your dreams and goals on paper, you set in motion the process of becoming the person you most want to be. Put your future in good hands—your own."

— Mark Victor Hansen

If you are looking out for a job, you should know what you want and in which position you fit in, based on your skills, interest, and probably your experience. You can create a usable resume only if you know what you want to do and what your goal is.

You should know what you want to do in life and what direction you want to have in your career. Your resume should contain the appropriate information to back up this self-assessment.

3.2 Not Writing for the Audience

One of the major mistakes when creating a resume is not understanding the needs or interests of the people (the hiring managers or potential employers), who would be reading your resume. When you start working on any document—book, article, presentation, e-mail, resume—the most important question you have to ask is, "*Who am I writing for*?"

The answer to this question is the deciding factor for the appropriate language, content, tone, organization, structure, and style for your writing. Readers have expectations from the document they read and hence certain details have to be included or excluded.

Example: *Students referring to a textbook or a reference book to learn more about the concepts of refraction and reflection will be interested in the examples cited with the help of the prism, but they will definitely not appreciate the information that describes the appearance of the prism.*

Similarly, the people reading ***Femina*** *(the women's magazine) may not enjoy reading information on stock market or sports. The readers who have special interest in a particular subject will buy magazines which deal with that subject.*

Similarly, while writing your resume, you should anticipate the needs or expectations of the readers of the resume in order to convey appropriate information to them. If you do not know the expectations of the people reading your document, and you are not writing for them. You are probably writing for yourself, for the wrong person.

3.3 Not Serving the Purpose

According to research, during the initial shortlisting process, resumes are quickly scanned rather than read. So in all, you have a few seconds to impress and persuade a prospective employer to read the resume any further.

What this means is that the first impression of the resume is the deciding factor to get you an interview. Hence, the first few lines should catch the interest of the employers, impress them, and convince them of the your interest, qualifications, skills, and eligibility. Else, your resume will fail its purpose.

Take care of the following aspects so that your resume contains useful information and serves the purpose.

- Create separate resumes for different positions.
- Create separate resumes for similar positions requiring different skills (see Section 8.1).
- Highlight related skills, experience, and activities performed (see Section 8.8).
- Use action and power words (see Section 8.5).
- Give quantitative information (see Section 8.10).
- Keep it short, yet informative.

3.4 Writing Unwanted Information

Most of the time people add unwanted and irrelevant information such as, birth dates, sex, marital status, passport number, hobbies, religion, height, weight, father's name, mother's name, and their occupation. Except for the birth date, which gives an idea about your age, the rest of the information is irrelevant to the hiring managers. Most of these information makes it look like an application to a matrimonial request or an entry-form for a beauty pageant.

- Strictly avoid adding unwanted hobbies or interests like *chatting, surfing, or making friends* in the list of hobbies. It is very suggestive as to what you may do at work—chat, surf, and gossip with friends. Who would want to have such employees in their organization?

- Avoid non-relevant hobbies, interests, or responsibilities in favour of more relevant and meaningful information. During the personal interviews, you may talk about your hobbies or interests in detail.
- You may add hobbies that is related to the position you are applying for.

Example: *Gardening (as a hobby) makes sense to the recruiter if the position you are applying for has something to do with horticulture or agriculture. Reading and writing adds value if you are applying for the position of a technical communicator. In any case, these days written communication is a basic requirement for any job.*

Remember, a resume is not an autobiography of your life. It is an opportunity to focus on the requirements of the readers. Have a clear understanding of what the prospective employers are looking for in the candidates applying for the position and include the information about yourself that is relevant to the job and responsibilities to be handled.

3.5 Focusing on Existing Responsibilities

Do not focus just on the duties and responsibilities of the currently held position and the previous positions. Your resume should not only describe what you have done in your current or previous jobs, but should include the benefits of your efforts and contributions in brief. That is, discuss your accomplishments, not your responsibilities.

Every position has certain set of responsibilities associated with it, but it is not necessary that everybody fulfils them. The degree of accomplishment, in terms of fulfilling the responsibilities or anything else varies drastically. Recruiters and prospective employers are primarily interested in the value you have brought to your previous or current employers.

Job descriptions in different organizations are never the same. They vary. So, it is necessary to modify the resume to showcase the skills and responsibilities the employer is expecting from you. You may have to make some rearrangement in the resume by moving around the sections, changing certain keywords or phrases, and restructuring the employment details.

Example: *A person working in administration department in an organization may have different responsibilities than a person working in another organization.*

In one organization, the person may be wholly responsible for handling the travel requirements (visa, hotel booking, air booking, other travel arrangements, etc.) of the employees going overseas. In the other, the administrative executive might have to take care of house keeping activities, take care of the facilities, canteen activities, and office maintenance related work.

3.6 Forgetting How?

If you can add more information in your resume, don't omit to mention how you have performed the tasks and activities. Telling your reader how you achieved your various successes allows them to get a better idea of your ability, capability, and knowledge. You don't need to write a thesis about it, a phrase or a sentence will do.

Example: **Avoid:** *Increased annual sales by 45%.*

Better: *Increased annual sales by 45% by implementing improved marketing techniques.*

The first statement does not portray your abilities and achievements. The second statement offers a stronger indication of value and success. In fact, it actually illustrates two achievements: increased sales and improved techniques.

While most of the how it was done information is best left to the interview stage, some of it needs to be mentioned in the resume. So, don't write lengthy paragraphs on how you went about doing your job—an indicator of the process followed should be enough. If the readers are interested in knowing more about it, they will ask you during the interview (telephonic or personal).

If you need help in determining the benefits of your contributions, ask yourself a few questions for each responsibility statement you list. For example, if you write "*I have 10 years experience in product development and have lead a team of programmers.*" Ask yourself the following questions:

- What are my roles and responsibilities in this position?
- Is this important?
- Why is this important to me?
- How did the efforts and contributions benefit me (in terms of productivity, production, profits, efficiencies, capabilities, costs, etc.)?
- What problems did I solve?
- What are the short and long-term benefit(s)?

3.7 Using Wrong Terminology

Most resumes receive an initial reading time of about 15 seconds or lesser. In such a situation, errors and wrong terminology makes you loose the chances of being shortlisted. You should also ensure to use the correct terminology for your position, responsibilities, and industry.

- Avoid using passive language, repetitive statements, change of tone or tense, and wrong terminology.
- Repetitive terms, such as *managed* is probably the commonly used word in the resumes. After reading about 20 resumes, the person shortlisting the resume will get bored and frustrated with the term, which otherwise is very impressive.

You may have managed many aspects of a project or the team. Even though *manage* is strong action word, it will loose its value if used repetitively throughout the resume. It can and should be varied with other action words which may be more accurate to the given situation. A little variation in terms keep the pace of reading and makes it interesting.

Example: **Avoid:** *I managed the people, managed the project, and managed the team.*

Better: I ***mentored*** *the new comers,* ***lead*** *the project, and* ***supervised*** *the team.*

3.8 Writing Lengthy Resumes

If you think that the hiring managers are patiently going to read your resume from the start till the end to understand the contents of your resume, you are mistaken. Hiring managers receive hundreds of resume for a single position. They spend a few seconds glancing through the resume to check if it fullfills the criteria they have asked for in terms of educational qualification, experience, and/or the required skill sets. Those few seconds are critical as the recruiters try to decide if you are to be considered at all.

Your resume is your marketing material, and so it is important to present the information such that it captures the interest of the readers quickly and that interest should stay on till they finish reading your resume.

- You should give the reader the information they are interested in, early in the document.
- This increases the chance for a more detailed reading.
- The resume should invoke interest of the hiring managers. Only then will they call you for a telephonic interview or a personal interview. Else, the resume will probably find its place in the recycle bin.
- The format of the resume should be such that most of the information can be located in a glance.

3.9 Not Organizing Properly

As a recruiting manager, I have come across many types of resumes:

- Resumes that run into pages containing invalid, unwanted, and useless information.
- A short one page resume, but not organized effectively and efficiently.
- One page short and crisp resumes that contain all the necessary information required to consider the candidate. [*Best resume*]
- Lengthy resume that is organized, structured, and formatted such that it is easy to locate the information and keywords in a glance. [*Second best resume*]

Spend some more time creating your resume so that valid information is visible to the recruiters during the first few seconds when they glance through it. You will be able to do it if you give some more importance to the organization of the information and the format of the resume. Organize the information such that it effectively highlights and showcases you skills, achievements, and accomplishments.

Another trick is to create a brief job summary at the beginning of your resume highlighting your skills and expertise. Ensure that the reader understands that the skills allow you to excel in your field and the position you hold. You may add the achievement that set you apart from the other candidates who may have similar skills and expertise as you. For details see Section 8.7, Organize the Information.

3.10 Not Focusing on the Employer's Needs

Your resume will either make you or break you. That is why you have to treat it as an advertisement about yourself. Most of the people buy the best advertised product than the best product. In the same way, if the resume catches the eyes of the prospective employer, they might give you a chance to prove your worth (in the interview or test).

Hiring managers would want to recruit candidates having the relevant experience, skill set, knowledge, and/or attitude. They would want people who fits well in the existing team. You have to write a resume to appeal directly to them.

- **Freshers:** When you seek a job in a field you know about, you are aware of the basic skills required for the position. If you do not know anything about the job, ensure not to make wild guess about the requirement.

  Get the required information from teachers, seniors, friends, online forums, books, and/or internet. Get a clear picture of what the employer is looking for in terms of job profile, responsibilities, and skills. Analyse what you have to offer before you begin creating your resume.

- **Experienced candidates:** If you have valid experience, you have a clear idea about what is expected of you in a similar position. You are also aware of the required skills and so you have to try to keep the need of the audience, (*i.e.*, managers, human resource) in mind when you create your resume.

  Give some thought and attention to the content and organization of the resume. If you are responding directly to the employer, analyse the job description and write accordingly.

To increase the effectiveness of your job-hunting process, learn to write an effective and dynamic resume, but do not make any claims that are not true. With a little thought, a little extra effort, and highlighting your skills and strengths efficiently, you can create an excellent resume. You can be assured to get a good response from prospective employers.

3.11 Not Customising the Content

Developing a good resume based on what you are is a challenging job. The educational background, employment needs, and the career objectives differ from individual to individual. Fine-tune your resume to the requirement of the position:

- If you are making a career change or if you are just out of college, you have to be especially careful in creating your resume. Highlight transferable skills (for career change) and soft skills (for freshers) because you cannot write about valid and relevant experience.
- If you are looking for a change in job, you have the relevant experience and the skill set to write about.
- If you are a fresher who has attended a certification course in the relevant field, you know the requirement of the job and the basics about the tools/software/scripting language used.

The resume should be tailor-made for the job, for you, and for the employer. It should convey the message to the prospective employer that you are a truly an exceptional candidate.

Example: *If you are simultaneously applying for the job of a design engineer and a quality assurance engineer, the resumes should have emphasis on different skill sets. You cannot use the same resume for both the positions.*

Some of the contents of the two can roughly be the same, but the objective, highlight and emphasis of the skill set should be different for both the positions.

3.12 Pretending, Fabricating, and Lying

All through this book, you are told that you have to grab the attention of the reader. True, but do not do it using gimmicks. Exaggerating or lying about experiences or achievements will make your resume effective or may help you in job search. But, fabricating professional history and achievements will have dire consequence.

So while fabricating may initially be of some benefit to you, the outcome can be devastating. You may get hired by giving false experiences and skills. It also gives false hopes to the employers. But will you be able to sustain in your new position, display your potential, and enjoy professional growth?

Your performance will speak about your real skills and expertise. Your employer will not take much time to find out that you lied on your resume. Suddenly, you will find that they are critical about your performance because their expectations don't match your performance and they may look at you with sudden suspicion. For details, see Chapter 9, Fudging Resumes.

3.13 Commonly Made Mistakes

What you should not do when writing a resume is neatly as important as what you should do when writing one. Some of the commonly made mistakes are:

- **Creating lengthy resume**

  Try to keep your resume as short as possible. This does not mean that you have to omit information to abide to this rule. It means that though you have to give enough information to present a good idea about yourself, you have to learn to write in a concise, but in a short and effective manner.

- **Being unprofessional**

  A resume is a reflection of your personality and your professionalism. Avoid resumes that:

  — Does not contain the required information.

  — Is too lengthy, but does not contain any valid information.

  — Contains too much emphasise on the skills sets not specific to the position.

  — Contains errors.

  — Have unclear information.

  Such resumes portray you in bad light.

- **Starting sentences with I or my.**

  Omit "I" *(I did this, I did that, I am responsible for, I performed, I managed, I ...)* and "my" *(my duty, my responsibility, my performance, my work ...)* because they can make you seem self-centred and immature.

  Example: **Avoid:** *I performed the following activities:*

  Better: *Performed the following activities:*

- **Using unwanted references**

  Ideally you need to add names of 2-3 people to act as references for you. You are asked to provide professional and business references, not personal references (as usually required in a bank).

  — References should be people who have worked closely with you and can describe your professional skills and experiences.

  — Provide details of current references, not people you have worked with more than a decade back.

  — Don't give names of friends or managers from unrelated departments in your organization (with whom you are probably very friendly with).

  — Ideally, one of the references should be your current supervisor/boss.

  — Don't give references of a remote manager if you are working in the Indian office and have a manager located here. This shows that you are not in good terms with your local manager and/or the team members.

  As the potential references if they feel comfortable being your advocate. If they are hesitant, find someone else. Obtain current phone numbers where the references prefer to be contacted and times when they are most likely to be available.

- **Using cliches**

  Avoid using cliches. Do not describe yourself *as dynamic, result-oriented, or self-motivated* if you are not. The interview with the recruitment managers how dynamic and self-motivated you are. If you call yourself self-motivated, explain how or/and why in brief. For details, see Section 8.20, Let The Employer Decide.

- **Using too much of emphasis**

  Though it is okay to use emphasis by adding bold or italic text in one or two places in the resume, don't overdo it. Do not add it throughout the resume as they do not add any value to the appearance of the resume. It will make the resume look messy.

- **Using fancy fonts types**

  Use the commonly used formal fonts such as Aerial, Garamond, Helvetica, Tahoma, or Times Roman when creating your document. Do not try to catch the attention of the reader by using fancy font types. If you are applying for a creative job, some recruiters may be impressed, but many may not be. So play safe.

Chapter 4 Formatting The Resume

Resumes can be formatted in various different ways. This chapter introduces you to the different formats in which you can create your resume. It also discusses where, when, and how these formats should be used.

- ❐ **Section 4.1:** Chronological Resume
- ❐ **Section 4.2:** Functional Resume
- ❐ **Section 4.3:** Chrono-Functional Resume
- ❐ **Section 4.4:** Targeted Resume
- ❐ **Section 4.5:** Which Format to Use?

A lot of people are uncertain about the type of resume they should use when looking for a job—it could be a new job, or change in job, or change in career. Choosing the right format for a resume, boils down to the consistency and depth of skills and work experience you have accumulated so far in your career. It is also about how well the job you are seeking is aligned with your work experience. In general, there are four formats of resumes:

- Chronological
- Functional
- Chrono-Functional (mixed)
- Targeted

You should use a format that best highlights your job skills, accomplishments, and experiences. There are different formats that can be used when creating a resume. Determining which one is right for you is not an easy task as you may think it to be. Each one of them has a distinct set of advantages and disadvantages.

You have to choose a format based on a good understanding of yourself, the purpose of your resume, and your audience. It should highlight and best communicate your skills, accomplishments, and experiences to the employer.

4.1 Chronological Resume

The resume in which you list your work history in a chronological manner, actually reverse chronological, is called a chronological resume. It is also referred to as a traditional resume. It contains the work history in a reverse chronological sequence listing all your experience from most-recent to least-recent.

It is one of the most commonly used form of resume because it is easy to describe the jobs you have held and the job profile you had. This resume works well if you have a stable work history.

4.1.1 Who Should Use?

You can choose a chronological resume if you:

- Have educational qualification that is directly related to the job position that you are applying for.
- Are applying for a job within the same field.
- Have an impressive and stable employment history.
- Have a stable employment history, within a specific industry.
- Don't have unexplainable gaps in your employment history.
- Can state and prove your accomplishments and achievements.

4.1.2 Advantages

Some of the advantages of the chronological resume are as follows:

- If your more recent job experiences are aligned with the job that you are seeking. These job descriptions and job titles get highlighted in the chronological format.
- It is easy to follow the progression of your career. It uses a reverse chronological order, to list jobs in a time-line sequence.

XYZ Pvt. Ltd.

- Mar 2008 – Till Date : Associate Manager Development
- Feb 2004 – Mar 2008 : Team Leader, Development
- Feb 2002 – Feb 2004 : Lead Engineer, Development
- Jan 2001 – Feb 2002 : Senior Engineer, Development

ABCD Ltd.

- Mar 2000 – Jan 2001 : Senior Engineer, Development
- Mar 1998 – Mar 2000 : Engineer, Development
- Apr 1997 – Feb 1998 : Trainee Engineer, Development

- The work experience summary section usually includes the following information:
  — The job titles you have had including your present designation.
  — The names of the organizations you have worked in.
  — The duration you worked at different organizations.
- You may add the responsibilities and work profile with the other information in the work details.
- It highlights the skills you had and the responsibilities you have handled in the organizations you have worked for in the past.
- It has a built-in time and so, it is more fact based. It also carries with it a lot of credibility in the eyes of the hiring manager or recruiter.

4.1.3 Disadvantages

The disadvantages of using the chronological resume are:

- Your work experience is listed in reverse chronological order. Any gap or break in your work experience time-line draws undue attention and stands out like a sore thumb.
- It allows the potential employers to clearly see that you have been switching jobs frequently. This is something most of the recruiters do not like in a prospective candidate.
- During a career change, a chronological listing of experience would make you look *over-qualified.*
- It distinctly shows your age. Though it is not a problem these days, it sometimes can be a big disadvantage for both younger and older job seekers (specially for those change in career).
- Any irregularities in your career path will be highlighted.

4.2 Functional Resume

A functional resume focuses and emphasises on your skills, qualifications, accomplishments, and experience. It does not focus on your work history or your designation. This format focuses attention on skills and achievements, rather than place of employment and the responsibilities you handled. Hence, it is ideal for people looking for change in career or fresh graduates looking for jobs. It is also useful for someone with little (or no) work experience.

4.2.1 Advantages

The resume works well if you have performed very similar activities throughout your past jobs who want to avoid repeating those activities in a chronological job listing. The advantages of the functional resume are:

- You can use it efficiently if you have gaps in your employment history.

  Example: *You may have taken time after child birth to take care of the child for 3-4 years and now wish to return to work.*

  A chronological format can draw undue attention to those gaps, while a functional resume enables you to portray transferable skills attained through such activities as domestic management and volunteer work.

- It allows you to haunt your skills and experiences which your employer must be interested in.
- It allows you to focus on the transferable skills (specially when changing careers). It helps you have diverse experiences that does not add up to a clear career path.
- It allows you to highlight the skills required by the employer. It is especially useful for freshers and college students with minimal experience and/or experience unrelated to the chosen career field. Try to include as much context as you can within each functional description. It will provide the employers with enough details and will give them a better idea of regarding your skills.

Example: *Anand chose* **leadership** *as one of his skills and listed the following experiences supporting his statement:*

* *Selected as College Cultural Secretary.*
* *Served as President of Cricket Club for three years. Organized three university tournaments.*
* *Served as Executive Member of Indian Student Association.*

In this example, Anand tells where he demonstrated each skill, thus making helping the employer connect his skills with the experience that produced those skills.

- You are changing your career, wishing to enter a field very different from your experience. That is, you have no related work experience.

4.2.2 Disadvantages

The disadvantages of using the functional resume are as follows:

- Many employers become suspicious at the sight of such resumes, as it hides spotty employment records.
- Some employers are not used to the functional format and they may become confused by the functional resumes.

4.3 Chrono-Functional Resume

A combination of the chronological and functional format is called a chrono-functional format. It is also called hybrid, combination, or mixed format. It first lists your skills and experience followed by your employment history. With this type of resume, you can highlight the skills you have that are relevant to the job you are applying for and also provide the chronological work history that employers prefer.

Some employers like to know what you did in each job. A solution is to structure your resume in a functional format but include one line statements of work history in reverse chronological order.

Such a work-history section need to include only job title, name and location of employer, and dates of employment. You do not need to list what you did in each job because that information will already be listed in the functional section.

4.3.1 Advantages

The advantages of using a combination resume is as follows:

- If you have handled the same kind of basic job responsibilities for a number of employers, you do not have to repeat them.
- If you are changing careers, you can focus the reader's attention on your skills and achievements.
- If you have a variety of work experience in unrelated fields, this format allows you to emphasize your abilities and skills rather than your employers and unrelated experience.
- If you are a recent college graduate, you can downplay your lack of employment by targeting other features, such as achievements, awards, and volunteer work.

4.4 Targeted Resume

A resume that is customized to highlight your experience and skills that are relevant to the job you are applying for is called a targeted resume. Though it takes more work and time to write a targeted resume, it is well worth the effort, especially when applying for a job that is a perfect match for your qualifications, skills, and experience. The easiest way to target your resume without rewriting the existing resume is to do the following.

1. Include some sections (according to your requirement) named:
    - Summary of work
    - Work history
    - Qualifications
    - Career highlights

2. Consider the experience, credentials, and education that best match the job posting and include them in the appropriate section in your resume.
3. List your experience in reverse chronological order, just as it is done in a traditional chronological resume.

4.5 Which Format to Use?

Chronological format is the most commonly used for most of the resumes. These days, the other formats are also used depending on the purpose of the resume and various other factors. When deciding which format to use, ask yourself the following questions:

- Are you a first time job seeker?
  - Have you just finished a graduate degree?
  - Are you a graduate looking for your first job a few years after graduation?
- Are you looking to change job, career, or industry focus?
- Have you changed jobs too often?
- Are you seeking a promotion within your organization?
- Are you looking at a senior position within your field at another organization?
- Does your resume allow the interviewer to ask you enough questions?
- Are you planning to relocate?
- Are you returning to work after a gap of 2-3 years (maternity leave, family problems, or medical problems)?

The answers to these questions will help you determine which format you should use.

Chapter 5

Contents of a Resume

Writing a targeted and effective resume is difficult and time-consuming, but it will not be as difficult if you know what you have to write. The most important thing to remember is that there is no one right way to do it. First and foremost you should know about the components of the resume.

People write resumes for various reasons. The most common one is to apply for jobs/change in job, the first job, after college, sometimes for promotions, etc. Whatever your reason for writing a resume, the basic purpose of the resume remains the same/to communicate your experience, skills, and education related to a specific position to an employer.

Writing a great resume does not necessarily mean that you should follow a set of rules, because there is no right way of writing a resume. It depends on your background, employment needs, and the career objectives. Ideally, you can divide the resume into a few standard sections:

- Objective
- Educational qualification
- Skill set
- Other skills/details
- Seminar/conferences: In this section, list the seminars and conferences you have attended and/or participated in. Also mention any short-term courses or certification you have done.
- Publication: Mention any articles published in the newspaper or in some magazine. If the number of articles or publication is about five in number (or less), write a brief introduction about them. Otherwise, the list will suffice.
- Professional experience
- Contact Information
- Personal information

5.1 Objective

A well-defined objective adds a great deal of value to the resume as it demonstrates your clarity of career direction. An objective for name sake adds no value and an objective that does not match with the requirement can be a royal disaster.

A well written objective gets the person's attention and interest. This first few sentences of the resume conveys a very important and powerful message—*I want the very job you are offering, and I am the most suitable candidate because I understand the qualities that you consider to be important for the job, and most importantly I have them.*

This message that comes through the objective can do wonders because:

- The employer will know that someone who wants to do exactly what they are offering will be much more likely to succeed than someone who doesn't. So you stand more chances of being called for an interview.
- The employer will know that it is easier to work with a person who knows the expectations of a job.
- If you have done a good job of establishing, then you are the perfect candidate in the first sentence, it shows that you have thought about the qualities that makes you stand out from the rest. You have already started putting in the effort in the right direction.

Being on the other side of the hiring table has taught me that many people actually miss getting an interview because of a wrong objective. Even if you are a perfect fit for the position in terms of the level of experience and job profile, your objective might let you down. So, unless and until you have a clear and well-defined objective statement, it is better not to have one at all.

Example: *If you are responsible for short listing the resumes for the post of a web developer and you come across the a list of objectives as shown in Figure 5.1, who would you consider?*

This is assuming the fact that you are going to read the resume based on your interest after reading the objective.

1. To work with a reputed organization and be able to apply CAD software and mechanical design skills for delivering challenging projects.
2. To be associated with a firm that provides me an opportunity to grow by acquiring new skills and thus contributing toward the development of the firm and myself.
3. Seeking a challenging position in a competitive environment involving analysis, design and development of mechanical hardware/software systems.
4. Seekiing a position of a trainee design engineer, wanting to become an established design engineer.
5. To obtain an entry level Engineering position in a dynamic, innovative, Mechanical company at the forefront of their field of expertise, a position that will enhance technical skills and allows opportunity for an advancement with the willingness to work hard and contribute to team goals.
6. Seeking the position that requires passion, enthusiasm, leadership and zeal to work in the field of design of mechanical machine elements.
7. To apply my programming skills in a fast growing organization where technical, hardworking, leadership, managerial skills would be needed.

Figure 5.1: A List of Objectives

I would consider No. 4 for having an objective that well connects with the job requirement. If I require one more resume, I might consider No. 2 because the objective is generic in nature. The other objectives do not match with the job requirement at all. In the bargain, I may loose out on a good candidate. The other way round, a good candidate might loose out on an opportunity because of the mismatch in the objective.

A well written objective gets the readers attention and interest. The first few sentences of the resume should convey a very powerful message—*I have the qualities that you consider is important for the position you have advertised. I am probably the most suitable candidate.* If your objective can convey this message across, you will surely be called for an interview because:

- You have done a good job of establishing why you are the perfect candidate. The interviewers know the qualities they want in a candidate. As soon as they read your resume they get a feel whether you are suitable for the position or not.

- It shows that you are an intelligent and thoughtful. You just have to prove yourself during the telephonic and/or personal interview.
- The interviewer is even smarter enough to know that someone who wants to do exactly what they are offering will be the most perfect match. Such a candidate is more likely to succeed in the position than someone who doesn't.

So, think clearly, create a good objective, and steer your career along a clear target that will meet your goals and interests and be professionally and personally satisfied.

5.1.1 Why Objectives Fail?

The objective fails for several reasons. The five most common reasons are:

- **It is too vague.**

  If the objective is specific, the persons reading the resume will get some idea regarding what the applicant is looking for and whether they want to consider the candidate.

  Example: *Consider an objective for the position of a trainee which states:*

  Seeking a challenging position in a competitive environment involving responsibilities that promotes growth.

  What is a *challenging position?* What does "*to promote growth*" mean? Having responsibilities will not promote growth. How you handle the responsibilities and how you perform them? Such phrases are too vague and does not add value to the objective or the resume.

- **It does not justify why you have applied for the job.**

  There are times when you may be desperate to do any kind of work, in the need of a job (not a career). In such cases, even if you are not sure about what you are looking for do not let this uncertainty show anywhere in the objective. Always give an explanation why you have applied for a particular position and how you fit in.

As a trainee, your focus should be about getting trained, learning the required skills, and the job processes.

— If you are applying of a junior position, the resume must be specific to that position, with an appropriate objective and skill sets.

— If you happen to be a fresher, justify how you would be capable of handling the job-related activities.

— If you have about 3-4 years experience, explain why you have applied for a junior position.

If you are able to display that you are capable, you will get to handle responsible tasks, activities, and projects.

- **It is not related to the position applied for.**

The objective should be specific to the position you are applying to. Else, instead of grabbing the attention of the reader, you will be responsible for loosing it.

Example: *Consider a resume for the position of quality testing engineer having an objective that states:*

Seeking the position that requires passion, enthusiasm leadership, and zeal to work in the field of design of mechanical machine elements.

This overview has nothing to say about the interest or inclination towards testing. The rest of the resume may be specific to the job, but the person sorting the resume may not to look at the rest of the resume after reading this objective.

- **It talks about what you want.**

Don't make the mistake of mentioning your dream in your objective. It should be specific to the job and to the requirement of the interviewer. During the interview, you may tell the interviewer about your expectations and what you would like to do. But there is no need to declare it in the objective—just mention what you want to do for the applied position, and how you fit in!

- **It is too self-centred.**

  Objective should never be written from a self-centred point of view. Even when people have a specific objective, they often make it self centred.

  Example: *Seeking a challenging position where I can hone my skills, gain experience, and get opportunity for advancement in career.*

  It is a well known fact that people change jobs to earn better salary, to acquire varied skills and to fullfill their dreams and aspirations. But are these the only objectives? Most of the employers are interested in hiring you for what you can do for them, not to help you to fulfil your goals. They would expect you to join in an institute to hone your skills.

5.2 Educational Qualification

If you have a string of degrees and diplomas to boast of, you can add them under a separate section. If you have a lone degree, do not have a separate section to mention it. Add it in the **Personal Information** section.

- List education in reverse chronological order.
- List selected course work if this will help convince the reader of your qualifications for the targeted job.
- Include advanced training, with selective and summarized information, including only what would be of any interest to the reader.
- If you have working experience of more than 5 years, you do not have to mention your grades (or per cent of marks).

5.3 Skill Set

Focus on the strongest and most impressive skill sets. Make careful and strategic choices to organize, order, and convey your skills. If you are applying for a position in software industry, you may add the following information in this section:

- The operating systems you work on.
- Any programming language you know.
- List of the package and tools you have used.

If there is a large set of tools, you can have them under separate headings. The skills should be specific to the job applied. If you are applying for the position of a documentation engineer, ensure that you add the appropriate skills (see Examples 1 and 2).

Example 1: Operating Systems: UNIX, Windows 4.0

Languages: Java, C, C++

Internet Technologies: XML, ASP, HTML, JavaScript

Methodologies: Object Oriented Analysis and Design (OOAD)

Example 2: Packages and Tools: FrameMaker 7.0, InterLeaf, LATEX PowerPoint, HTML, MS Word, DreamWeaver, Photoshop

Text Editors: Java Editor, Xemacs

Conversion Tools: WebMaker and Webworks (FrameMaker to HTML)

Operating Systems: UNIX, Windows

Internet Technologies: XML, ASP, HTML, JavaScript

Languages: Java, C, C++

Here, Example 1 contains all impressive skills but they are of little importance to the documentation team. The skill sets listed in Example 2 is valid and important as it contain the information about packages, tools, text editors, and conversion tools. Hence, it will be more appealing to a person who is reading the resume.

5.4 Other Skills/Details

In this section you can list the optional skills you want to highlight. Do not club them in a paragraph or scatter them under various sections, where they get lost in the text.

List them out so that the person reading your resume can read these skill sets you have while glancing through the resume.

- Accumulate all of your miscellaneous skills in this section. You can add statements like:
  - Ability to describe complex technology clearly and concisely.
  - Can learn new tools and processes without much direction.
- Add some personal information like professional associations, professional memberships, and hobbies.
- Add information specific to area of interest:

  Example: *Consider a resume for the position of a QA engineer that contains the following information:*

  Area of Interest: *CAD-CAM, Software development, GUI design, Developing Website.*

  The area of interest listed here will only put the manager or the person going through the resume on defense since it talks about CAD-CAM and developing Website, but nothing related to the job applied for.

5.5 Professional Experience

List your experience in the reverse chronological order.

- If you have worked with a number of organizations, do not go into details about the jobs early in your career.
- Focus on the most recent and/or relevant jobs.

- Summarize the earliest jobs in one line or very short paragraph with a brief of your job summary and achievements of any.
- If the list of experience is limited, you can write a little more elaborately, about your job profile and responsibilities.
- The jobs listed should include the designation, the name of the firm, and the number of years you have been with them.

5.6 Contact Information

This information is used to identify who you are, and where you are from, and make it as easy as possible for the employer to reach you.

Bipasha. R. Basu

bipashabasu@company.co.in

Current Address:	**Permanent Address:**
House No. 20	Flat No. 17
Main Street, Kothrud,	Shashi Marg, Avadi,
Pune, Maharashtra,	Chennai, TN
Mobile: 0123456789	**Mobile:** 1234567890
Landline: 020-12345678	**Landline:** 044-12345678
bipashabasu@yahoo.com	*bipashabasu@yahoo.com*

- **Name**

  Give your formal first and last name (*Rahul Gandhi*). You may also include your middle name (*Sanjay Leela Bansali*) or initial (*Bipasha. R. Basu*) if you like.

- **Address**

  Give your complete address of where are located presently. If you are working in Pune, don't give a Chennai address (where your parents reside). This will give a wrong idea about your present location.

You may also give both the addresses (current address and permanent address) so that it becomes clear where you are actually from and where you are currently located.

- **Telephone Numbers**

  Always list your telephone numbers that is easily assessable. Most companies prefer the convenience of contacting applicants by phone during day time.

  — If you have roommates, let them know when employers might be calling you so they can answer the phone appropriately and take or give messages.

  — If you have an answering machine or voice mail, make sure you have an appropriate message for greeting employers.

  — If you are not in a position to take calls during the day time, mention why. If possible, mention a small duration (10-15 minutes) in the day time when they can call you to arrange for further discussions.

- **E-mail Addresses**

  Include your preferred e-mail address, that is an e-mail address you are able to check on a daily basis during your job search. If you have more than one e-mail accounts, you can list all of them. Ensure that they are appropriate and professional addresses.

- **URL Addresses**

  If you have a well-maintained resume in a professional looking personal site or a work site (if you are a freelancer) on the web, include the URL on your resume. This can be particularly important for those seeking careers in web design or related fields.

5.7 Personal Information

The section on personal information should ideally contain your name, phone number (including the daytime number), e-mail address, correspondence address, and the URL to your home page or blog if you have one.

Name :	Suraj Kapoor
Father's Name :	Raj Kapoor
Sex :	Male
Date of Birth :	10 March 1980
Marital Status :	Married
Nationality :	Indian
Height :	165 cm
Weight :	66 kg
Education :	B.Sc. (Chemistry)
Language Known :	English, Hindi, Marathi, Kannada
Passport No. :	A-70441667

Most of the time this section contains unwanted and irrelevant information such as, birth dates, sex, father's name, marital status, passport number, height and weight. Is this information going to be of any use to the recruiters? Except for the name of the candidate, the rest of the information is irrelevant. Most of these information makes it look like a matrimonial form or an entry-form for a manhunt competition or beauty pageant.

- You can mention your age, but birth date is irrelevant information to the person who is reading the resume.
- Mention your passport number if you applying for a job abroad because the recruiters may want to verify the detail, but otherwise avoid adding such information unless and until it is specifically asked for.
- You may add some personal information like professional memberships and hobbies as a separate section in the end of the resume.
- If you don't have a string of degrees or diplomas, you can add them in this section against the heading Education. Else, educational qualification has to be written under a separate section.

Chapter 6
An Electronic Resume

Many people still think that the resume you upload online is not the same as the one you create to mail to prospective employers. This is untrue.

You do not need a different resume, you only need to alter the format of your existing resume to make it easy for you to post by copying and pasting in the job sites. This chapter discusses the following topics:

- ❒ **Section 6.1:** What is Electronic Resume
- ❒ **Section 6.2:** Resume Versions
- ❒ **Section 6.3:** Preparing A Plain Text Resume
- ❒ **Section 6.4:** Guidelines—Responding Online
- ❒ **Section 6.5:** Staying Cyber-Safe

6.1 What is Electronic Resume?

An electronic resume (e-resume) is designed specifically for use on a computer. It can be:

- Distributed via e-mail.
- Uploaded on the intranet.
- Searched for keywords located by search engines.
- Converted into other electronic file types.
- Saved on a computer hard drive or CD.
- Printed to paper when required.

The printed resumes that are send by post have become extinct. As a hiring manager, in the last nine years I have received only one printed resume via postal mail. I think, while selecting jobs, even the candidates are choosy and do not respond to the advertisements that give an address where the candidates are supposed to send their resumes by post.

You can mail the resume in many formats:

- In the body of the mail. This is no longer a preferred or efficient method because the resume cannot be saved or stored in a folder. Do this only if the advertisers specifically ask you not to send an attachment.
- Plain text format. It be in .txt or .rtf format.
- MS Word document. It is the most popular format.
- PDF format. It can not be tampered with, but the readers can read it using Acrobat Reader.

6.2 Resume Versions

It is recommended to keep duplicate versions of your resume in each of the following versions or formats.

- **Print Version:** Such format is designed and well-formatted with bulleted lists, italicized and bold text, and other highlights. This is usually prepared as a MS Word document and is ready to be send as an e-mail attachment or to be printed to hand to potential contacts and interviewers.

- **Scannable Version:** It is a document that has been formatted in such a way that all the information can be easily scanned and loaded into electronic programs that are operated with the use of optical character recognition software.

  This format does not have any fancy design highlights. Though bulleted lists are acceptable, it is not an automated format. That is limited to the use of a dash (–) or a star (*). This type of resume can be in .rtf or .txt format.

- **Text Version:** A plain text file is useful as you can copy and paste the information into online forms or post it in the online resume databases.

- **E-mail Version:** It is another plain text copy, but is specifically formatted for the length-of-line restrictions in e-mail. It is send out in the body of the e-mail.

You actually do not have to spend a lot of time creating all these versions of the resume. You need to prepare one document, preferably in MS Word and then you can convert them to different formats. You have to spend sometime in adding format (like dash or star for the bulleted items) for the text and e-mail versions of the resumes.

6.2.1 Why Plain Text?

In most of the job sites, you may be asked to use the forms provided by most of the databases to build your resume in their system. Having a resume in text format will help you in the following:

- **Spell-check:** Preparing your resume using your own word processing program allows you to spell-check your resume and revise until you are happy with it.
- **Format:** Most online forms insist on a chronological resume, which focuses on work history. You can pick and choose information from the text format and use it here without any extra formatting efforts.

- **Reusability:** Different job sites have different formats. If you have to build a resume with all the information that is asked for in text format. You will not have to repeat your effort for every database where you want to add your resume. You can easily copy and paste the relevant area in the online resumes.

6.3 Preparing A Plain Text Resume

Preparing your resume for online purposes or to be sent via e-mail is really an easy process. Most word processors will let you save the resume in plain text format. You just need to take the extra few minutes to generate a plain text version and alter the format to make it more user-friendly. You have to make sure that you do the following:

- Check that the resume is a continuous document.
- Remove any information (like page number, name of the candidate, etc.) that is usually available in the footer or header of the word format.
- Replace the bullet mark with a standard keyboard symbol. Suggested replacements are:
  - Dashes (–)
  - Plus signs (+)
  - Single asterisks (*)
  - Double asterisks (**)

  You may use different symbols to represent different formats, example lists, and lists in lists.
- Use the **Space** bar, not the **Tab** key. You may have to check if tabs have been used for indentation.
- The tabs and tables used in the word document will disappear. So, look out for extra spaces because items that were once in columns and tabular format are now in paragraph format.
- Before sending your resume in text format to an employer, send it to yourself to see how it looks when you receive

it. This will help you identify any formatting problems you need to consider before you send it to possible employers.

6.4 Guidelines: Responding Online

The fastest way to respond to a job is to e-mail your cover letter and resume to the person who has advertised the position. Remember you have a few seconds to make a stranger open the e-mail, open your resume, scan through it, and shortlist it. There are chances that even after all the efforts you have taken to create a wonderful resume, it may get rejected, the mail may get deleted, and find its way to the trash folder.

Getting your e-mail read and actually considered boils down to the following rules:

6.4.1 Use the Right Subject

Avoid vague subject line which says anything that does not interest the recipient to open and check the resume. Use the job title or job code cited in the advertisement.

Example: **Avoid:** *Hi, Resume, Rucha Kumar, Seeking employment*

Better: *Design Engineer (5 years exp)*

If the HR person is sorting numerous e-mails for various position, it becomes easy to route your mail to the appropriate person based on the subject line.

6.4.2 Follow Instructions

If you are responding to an advertisement, read the instructions and follow them.

- If there are multiple position, you may be asked to use a specific e-mail address for a specific job position. Do not assume that since the advertised positions are for the same organization, you can send your resume to any of the e-mail addresses listed there. If you think that the HR will do the job of forwarding the mails to the appropriate department, you are mistaken. They have other duties and responsibilities to perform.

- If the advertisement asks you to refer to a job code for a specific job function in the subject line or use a specific subject line, do it. The HR personals may sort the resumes based on the subject line, put them in different folders, and send them to the respective hiring managers.
- In some cases, the advertisement might have a note asking you to not to send an attachment or might ask you to send only a word attachment.

  When the instruction is not to send out an attachment, don't do it. Don't force someone to open an attachment when they don't want to do it. Chances are no one will open it.

In short, read the instructions and follow whatever they want you to do. Failing to follow the instructions, labels you as someone who doesn't take direction and/or instructions well and does not perform as instructed. It may also come accross as if you have not understood the instructions. Chances are, you will be rejected outright.

6.4.3 Check the Format

Make sure your resume is properly formatted in text format. Plain text resumes, if not formatted, will not be readable. Such resumes are most likely to be deleted. Who wants to take time and effort to figure out what has been written in the resume.

You are the person who has to put in time and effort to ensure that your resume looks good and well-formatted. Ensure to have shorter text lines, spacing between sections, and text-based highlights (bold or italics).

6.4.4 Add an Introduction

If you are sending your resume as an attachment, include a brief introduction about yourself in the mail. Most of the time, people send an e-mail with an attachment with various subject lines like

My resume, *Subhash Roy's resume, Your advertisement,* or a simple *Hi* with just attachment and no text in the body of the mail.

These days, with so many issues with viruses, on one will be inclined to open an attachment sent by an unknown person. A brief paragraph about yourself, your qualification, and experience will encourage the person to read your resume.

Always remember just as it is easy for you to click the send button and send out the resume, it is easy for someone else to click the delete button and delete it.

6.5 Staying Cyber-Safe

Web privacy is an oxymoron. You can not put some document or information on the web and expect privacy. So, first and foremost decide if you want to put up your resumes online in a job database or job site. If you have decided to go ahead with it, do it with care. Be careful about the information presented in the resume and upload them only on selected job sites.

6.5.1 Limit Your Postings

Post your resume in the databases of only in a few popular job sites. This will help you in the following ways:

- *Maximum exposure:* You will have access to many employers across industries and regions.
- *Targeted exposure:* If you are very specific about the area of work, post it in the databases of one or two smaller job sites targeted to your specific occupational group or industry. You will have access to employers looking at a focussed and appropriately qualified and dedicated candidates.

6.5.2 Registration

First check if the site allows you to search the job database without registering or putting up your full resume. If it does, you may go ahead and evaluate the site to make sure whether you want to add your resume to their database.

You should be allowed to evaluate a site to make sure it is a good fit to you before adding your information to their database. If it doesn't, look for another that does.

As far as possible, avoid job sites that allows you to search the job database only after registering or putting up your resume.

6.5.3 Contact Information

If you are not sure about the credibility of the job sites, don't add information regarding any of your contact information. You may enter your e-mail address, but don't add information such as phone numbers or mobile numbers. If some one wants to contact you, they will write to you and then if you are interested, you can give them your contact numbers/information.

6.5.4 Renew Your Resume

Many job database sort resumes by date of submission. That probably means the newest resume is displayed first. If you do not get any response to your resume within 15-30 days, try updating, reformatting, and submitting your resume again. You may also post your resume elsewhere. There could be a possibility that:

- Employers are not looking for people with your skills in a particular database.
- There is too much competition between candidates with the same skills and probably, your resume is not catching the interest of the recruiters.
- Your experience does not match the requirement.

6.5.5 Remove Your Resume

When your job search is over, delete your resume from the database. You may be tempted to wait to see if something better might come up. But remember you have just joined an organization (or another organization). Concentrate on the job, prove yourself, and try to become a valuable employee. You may not want your current employer to find your resume still floating/circulating in the job sites.

Chapter 7

Cover Letter

A resume is often the first line of contact which establishes a first impression of the skills, background, and hiring value of a potential job candidate. If it is well-written, it may convince the reader that the you are ideally suited for the job. When coupled with an effective cover letter, the resume can be a very strong marketing tool. Hence, when sending your resume, ensure to include a cover letter to explain why you are sending it. This chapter discusses the following topics:

- **Section 7.1:** What Is It?
- **Section 7.2:** Purpose
- **Section 7.3:** Contents of a Cover Letter
- **Section 7.4:** Parts of a Cover Letter
- **Section 7.5:** Guidelines—Cover Letter
- **Section 7.6:** Do's and Don'ts

7.1 What Is It?

A cover letter is an essential part of your correspondence with an employer in your search for a job. A well-written cover letter can result in the difference between a quick glance or a careful reading of your resume. While the resume provides an overview of your background, the cover letter allows you the opportunity to highlight those aspects of your background that are relevant to the position you are seeking.

A good cover letter will help in developing the employer's interest in your profile. Some employers are interested in knowing why you have applied for the job. A resume requires good writing and attention to detail, but a cover letter demands even more—it is addressed to a particular person who is in charge of hiring. It requires you to address the most important question that is in the mind of the interviewers—*why are you the best suited for the job?*

Success is never found at the top of the hill, if the duties at the foot are neglected.

— **Eva Arringtom**

7.2 Purpose

The purpose of a cover letter is not to get you the job, but to complement the resume and to improve your chances of being called for an interview. Instead of having a telephonic interview, chances are you might be directly called for an face-to-face interview. That is why it pays to learn the most effective strategies for writing cover letters. All cover letters should do the following:

- **Explain why you are sending a resume.**

  Don't make the reader guess what you are asking for. Be specific. As far as possible, send a resume along with a cover letter. A cover letter is a personal letter explaining the following:

— Why you are applying for the position.

— Why you are looking for a change.

— Your interest in the position.

— Your interest in the organization.

- **Tell how you learned about the position.**

  You have to mention how you came to know about the position in the organization. It could be through an advertisement in the newspaper, job advertisement on a bill board, on a job site, or through the website. If you came to know about the position through a friend who works at the organization, you may mention the name of the person who suggested that you write.

- **Convince the reader to look at your resume.**

  The cover letter is a summary of your resume. It tells the prospective employer:

  — Who you are.

  — What your interest is.

  — What your accomplishments are.

  — Your interest in the job.

  If written and presented in the right manner, the cover letter will add immense value to your resume. Therefore, it must be very well-written and targeted to that employer.

- **Pay attention to the important aspects.**

  A good cover letter addresses the queries the recruiters have about education, skills, leadership, knowledge, and experience that are relevant to a position you are seeking. It should also reflect your attitude, personality, motivation, enthusiasm, and communication skills.

- **Provide information that cannot be included in a resume.**

  Add any information specifically requested in the job advertisement that might not be covered in your resume, such as:

— Availability date

— Reason for change of job.

— References to any blogging site to show off your writing skills.

7.3 Contents of a Cover Letter

The cover letter should contain a concise summary of your interest, experiences and skills. It is an attempt to influence and justify why the company should hire you.

A good cover letter demonstrates your creative talent, insight, and the communication skills. Ideally it should include the following information:

- A brief summary of your career so far (if you have relevant experience)
- A summary of your interests and skills that is relevant to the position (if you a fresher).
- An overview of the type of job you are now looking for. This will help the recruiters shortlisting the resumes to decide if you would be interested in the type of the job they will have to offer you.
- Preferences regarding location, unless you are open to relocation.
- Your salary expectations, if it is an important criteria for you. If not, it is best to avoid such information.

7.4 Parts of a Cover Letter

The contents of a cover letter can be divided into three main parts: introduction, body, and closing paragraph. See Figure 7.1

7.4.1 Introduction

The first paragraph should introduce yourself and state two reasons:

- How you came to know about the position.

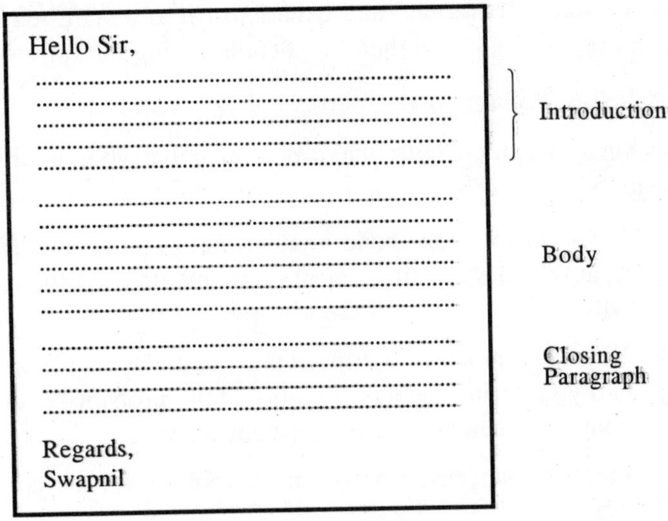

Figure 7.1 : Parts of a Cover Letter

- — If you have heard about a vacancy, mention how you heard of it.
- — If you are referred by someone, mention who has referred you.
- — If you came to know about the position from an advertisement, mention the source; newspaper, online forum, job sites, etc.

- Why you are suitable for the position. Explain this in brief and keep it short (say about a paragraph). But ensure that it attracts enough attention to entice the reader to want to read the rest of the letter.

7.4.2 Body

The main body of your letter can be one or two paragraphs long. It should contain some information regarding how you can contribute to the department. This paragraph is critical as it should convey the main idea of your responsibilities, the main projects you have worked on, your accomplishments, and anything else which is important but does not find place in your resume.

The information should interest the recruiters and should motivate them to meet you and talk to you. So you may mention a few key aspects of your background and experience if any. You may also mention that you can give them the details during the interview.

7.4.3 Closing Paragraph

The closing paragraph must make it clear about your interest in the position.

- If you have a telephone number that you cannot respond to during the day time, mention it and also add the reason why.
- You may mention a timeframe when the recruiters can call you during the day for a brief talk, probably to decide when you can have a longer conversation.
- Mention the reason why you are looking for a change of job.

7.5 Guidelines—Cover Letter

You have to follow certain guidelines when creating cover letter for your resume. These days resumes are usually sent and received via e-mail. The recruiters might prefer to save the resumes in .doc, .pdf, or .txt format in a folder for future references.

So sending the cover letter as a separate file or the text of the e-mail will be of a great a discomfort for the people maintaining the resume database. The information should be in one document instead of having a separate files for cover letter and resume.

While there are many ways of writing a great cover letter, there are some things that everyone should consider. Here are some tips on making your cover letter look professional.

- **Don't write it for the heck of writing it.**

  If you have nothing to write in your cover letter, don't create it. Do not create a cover letter containing useless information just for the heck of it. Avoid writing such generic and useless cover letters.

> I take pleasure in sending my candidature for the post of design engineer in your esteemed organization. In order to enable you to assess my candidature, I am enclosing my detailed resume which highlights of my acadmic accomplishments.

If you have absolutely no idea of what to write in a cover letter, the best alternative is to include an introduction at the start of the resume, wherein you can write a brief summary of yourself or your job profile.

- **Personalize the letter.**

  These days, most of the advertisements on the jobsites and the mailing lists leave behind a contact name. Whenever possible address that person in your cover letter. It is far more connective than writing than just addressing them as madam or sir.

  Example:

  Avoid: *To whom it may concern,*
  Dear sir,
  Dear madam,

  Better: *Dear sir/madam,*
  Dear Ms. Maya,

- **Do not be overly humble.**

  You should not be under confident or too humble. Your cover letter should show that you are confident enough to do the job, not that you are begging for one.

> I humbly request to check whether my credentials and your requirements match. I would deeply appreciate an opportunity for a personal discussion, through which you can evaluate the suitability of my candidature. I can assure you that I will measure up to your expectations. Please give me a chance to prove myself.

Such cover letters contain no added value and does not give any information about your interests or experience to the person reading it. Instead, it shows a pleading effect.

- **Be your natural self.**

  In your effort to impress the recruiters, don't try to sound like someone else. Don't use unnaturally formal language and words that you have never used before. Your aim might be to impress, but you may be awkward. Write as you would speak or a little better than that—many a times people write better than they speak.

  — Use simple, uncomplicated language and sentence structure.

  — Say things in simple, straight forward manner.

  — Use action words to form dynamic sentences.

  If you impress the interviewers by unfair means, like getting someone else write your resume or add wrong information about yourself, you might be called for the interview. But how will you impress them during the interview?

- **Draw attention.**

  Be honest, but not too modest. You have to try to draw attention to a particular skill or accomplishment that is important to the department and has meaning to the organization. Tailor your cover letter as much as possible to the requirements of the readers.

  Add information which will state how you are the right fit for the organization and what you can do for them instead of what they can do for your career. Including such information also shows that you have understood about the requirements and can fulfil them.

  Include some challenging information or thoughts that will pique the interest of the employer and will make them feel that it would be worth while to invite you for a discussion. Even if they really haven't been planning to hire anybody, they might want to talk to you and recruit you so that they don't loose a good prospective candidate.

- **Use appropriate language.**

  Try to create a cover letter without any mistakes. It means using awless language and avoiding the following:

  — Grammatical errors (use spell checker and proof read).

  — Using owery, dramatic, or pompous language (use simple language).

  — Complex and compound sentences (use active voice).

  — Jargon and heavy technical words (use short sentences).

  Avoid making statements like, *"I am enclosing my resume for your kind perusal."* Isn't that understood?

- **Be precise and specific.**

  The cover letter should be an introduction to the resume. It should not be repetitive—it should not contain information available in the resume. You can discuss the other skills during the interview. Remember that you are addressing a busy person. So try to ensure that the information is straight and clear.

  Make it clear as to why you are eligible for the job. Do not go into the details. If you do not have any experience and are looking for an opening to get into a particular field. You may write a paragraph describing:

  — What you like about the job profile?

  — Why you feel you are qualified for the job?

  — Why you are interested in the specific company?

  Though you may follow some tips and guidelines, the content of the cover letter should not be a Xerox copy of the resumes.

- **Be confident.**

  You should not be over-confident, arrogant, under-confident, or too humble. You should be confident.

  — Convey focused career goals.

— Mention how you are qualified and experienced for the position, but don't force it down their throat.

— Don't be too humble in your sign off. Avoid making statements like:

Example: Avoid making statements like:

I shall be eagerly waiting for your call. OR

Kindly consider my resume.

— Don't sound like you are begging for a job. The hiring managers will wonder why you are so desperate for a job.

- **Be positive**

Nobody wants to hire somebody with a negative attitude or someone who complaints about their work, boss, team members, or the organization:

— Do not complain about your current or past organization.

— Do not complain about your current or past boss or colleagues.

— Don't call the work as boring or tedious. Most of the time work is repetitive, and it is up to you to find ways of making it interesting.

— Do not say that the work was not challenging enough. Instead try to show that you have better skills and experience that were not properly utilized at all.

7.6 Do's and Don'ts

To create an effective cover letter, apart from the guidelines, you also have to follow ceratain do's and don'ts.

7.6.1 Do's

Here, we shall discuss what you should do and what a cover letter should be capable of doing.

Do's of A Cover Letter

A cover letter should do the following:

- Complement your resume.
- Be a condensed version of your experiences, skills, and knowledge.
- Address your cover letter to a specific person.
- Be specific about the position for which you are applying. Try to use the same language that was used in the advertisement.
- Be organized. Think of how you will present your information.
- Demonstrate enthusiasm.
- Be error free and perfect.

What You Should Do

You should do the following:

- Use appropriate titles, such as Dr., Ms., Mr., even though you know that several people will read your letter. If the advertisement does not specify any such details, use "Dear Sir/Madam" as the salutation. It is not necessary that the person reading your cover letter is a male.
- Ask someone whom you trust to read the final draft before you send it out.
- Edit, review, and proof read your cover letter a number of times till you are satisfied.
- Keep a copy of each cover letter you make, for your records.

7.6.2 Don'ts

The don'ts of a cover letter are:

- Do not duplicate your resume in your cover letter.
- Do not apply for jobs for which you are obviously not qualified and/or eligible.

- Do not begin with "*My name is...*"
- Do not ask rhetorical questions, such as "*Do you know why I would be a strong asset to your department?*"
- Do not use odd, ashy, or unusual fonts. Keep it simple.
- Do not exaggerate your qualifications or be dishonest.
- Do not write lengthy cover letters. It should not be more than one page.

Chapter 8

25 Tips for Creating Resume

Although there are many different styles and types of resumes, you should choose one that is unique to your experience and goals. Though creating a resume is a very important step towards getting a job, it is not taught at school or college levels.

You have to understand the fundamentals of resume writing and follow certain guidelines as you plan, write, and review your resume. This chapter helps you with suggestions, tips, and guidelines to write an impressive resume.

8.1 Serve the Purpose

Your resume should serve the purpose. Hence, it should contain the information the recruiters are looking for. Your resume is not about you. It is about how you can meet the needs of your reader and why they should consider you for that position. The purpose is also the same. In mutual terms, it means, meet the needs of your readers and get you the job interview.

- You should have separate resumes for different positions you may apply for. This is especially true if you are applying for your first job and you have not yet decided the type of positions for which you are best qualified for and may want to keep your options open. In such situations, you will have to create several resumes that will effectively target each one of the position you are applying for.
- Identify how you have benefited your previous employers in the past. Take credit for your participation and accomplishments. While aspects of your background may seem minor or of little value to you, they may be seen as a valuable asset to those looking for such skills or traits.

The information you provide should be relevant and valuable to your reader's goals and interests. The cover letter, objective, the highlighted skills, and experience should be specific to the position and should help to serve the purpose.

8.2 Should be Visually Pleasing

In figure 8.1, we have two pictures of the same person. Which one of these attracts your attention, makes you notice it, and looks appealing you? Probably the one labeled B. That's because of the pleasing appearance. The one labelled A is with a normal day look, with no attention to the appearance. In the picture labelled B, some attention is paid to the appearance. It is more artistic and the picture is visually pleasing.

Similarly, a resume should also be visually pleasing and appealing to the readers. Avoid cluttered paragraphs where the readers have to wade through the text to try and figure out what they are supposed to read. Also avoid unreadable, squashed, and small font size that makes the readers squint.

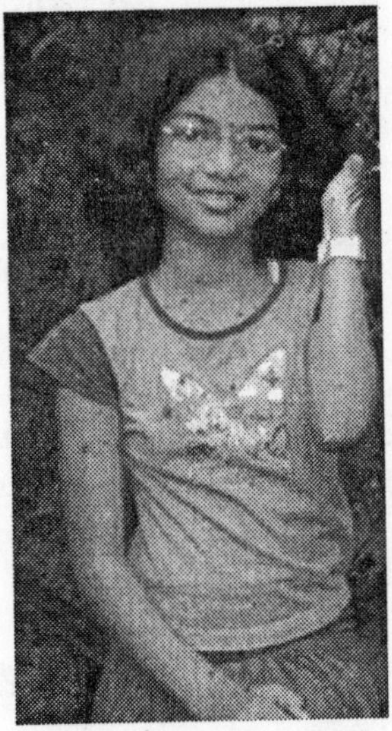

Appearance A

Appearance B

Figure 8.1: Appearences

The layout of your resume is extremely important. It should have a neat and professional appearance and should allow the reader access the information quickly.

8.3 Focus on Readability

The person reading your resume will not make efforts to try to find information that get lost in the paragraph even if they are specific to the skill-set or other important issues.

Hence, avoid large paragraphs as shown in Figure below which boast about the projects or work that you have done. You have to present to the readers the information that is easy to read. They should be able to scan your resume efficiently and effectively and easily locate the information they are looking for.

- Use lists and bullets to make the information stand out separately. Use bullets with short and crisp sentences to make it easier to quickly scan your resume and quickly locate the required information.

- Don't cramp in the information. Allow adequate white space.
- Use appropriate indentation to aid the ease of referencing the information.
- Do not use a font size that is smaller than 10 point.
- Use bold, all capitals, and italics fonts sparingly. Use them only when it is necessary to highlight something and use them consistently.
- Use symbols for numbers (#), dollar, ($) and percentage (%) as they stand out in the body of a resume.

Example: **Avoid:** *Increased sales by thirty-five percentage in south India in 2007.*

Better: *Increased sales by 35% in south India in 2007.*

Consider the placement of information in overall structure of the resume, location on the page itself or within a section, ordering of information, more impressive ways of phrasing the information, and use of design elements. Figure 8.3 splits the information appropriately into suitable paragraphs and lists. It is pleasing to the eye to have some space spread around in the document.

8.4 Be Clear

For every skill, accomplishment, or the job described, use the most active, accurate, and impressive verb you can think of.

- Use phrases rather than full sentences.
- Use commas to clarify meaning and make reading easier.
- Use words everyone can understand. Avoid using exorbitant and exquisite vocabulary.
- Start sentences with verbs, eliminating pronouns (I, he, or she).

Avoid	Better
• I have the ability to describe complex matter clearly and concisely.	• Ability to describe complex matter clearly and concisely.
• I can learn new tools and processes without much supervision.	• Can learn new tools and processes without much supervision.
• I have written articles on various topics in the newspaper.	• Written articles on various topics in the newspaper.

- Use recognizable industry keywords that will communicate to the hiring managers exactly where your expertise lies.

8.5 Use Power Words

A well-written and well-prepared resume will contain all of the necessary keywords to attract attention. The action words should be specific for an online resume and/or should be appropriate to be added into a resume system, indexed and searched online, or read on paper by a real human. For details, see Appendix B, Action Verbs.

Portray yourself as someone who is active, uses your brain, and gets things done.

- Use power words or verbs that match the level of position you are seeking. If you are applying for a senior position, show that you can manage projects and also supervise, mentor, and train people.

Example: **Avoid:** *Gave assignments to entry level writers and helped them get started with work.*

Better: ***Trained*** *and* ***mentored*** *the entry level writers.* ***Delegated*** *tasks to them, helped them get started and* ***supervised*** *their work.*

- Use lists that begin with action powered words like supervised, developed, co-ordinated, and achieved that best expresses your role and level of responsibility. Vary these terms to keep the pace of reading. This will add life to your resume.

8.6 Shorter is Better

The resume should not be too long or too wordy and should not run into pages. If you feel that the people are going to be impressed by a lengthy resume, you are sadly mistaken. The people shortlisting the resumes have to go through scores of resumes and will appreciate if the information is easily accessible to them at a glance.

- Avoid lengthy descriptions.
- Be concise and to the point.
- Keep sentences short and direct.
- Eliminate repetitions. If the positions you have held are similar, then it is unnecessary to repeating the same job functions in detail throughout your resume.
- Explain in the most direct way possible, rather than trying to impress with bigger words or complex sentences.
- Summarize the information so that resume length is kept short.

In addition to reviewing your experience, employers also use the resume to get a sense of whether you are organized, logical, and concise. Listing information that will be of no value to the position or company being targeted is just a waste of time.

8.7 Organize the Information

A well-written resume should reflect your personality as an organized writer. You may have all the skills required for the job, but if you don't present it properly in the resume, the chances are that you will not be shortlisted at all. Compare Figures 8.2 and 8.3 to understand why one is better than the other.

Worked from Aug 1997-98 (1 year)

Company: XYZ India Ltd.

Designation was Senior Development Engineer

Nature of Job was to development of Electronic Hardware For Computer Controlled Instruments/Systems.

The Automatic Compression Testing Machine is a computer controlled machine that is used in cement houses to measure the strength of concrete samples. The software provides a graphical interface to the operator of the machine with various options to conduct test runs, save test data, perform analysis on the saved data, manage data files and operator information. Apart from developing the Electronic Hardware for this machine, I was also responsible for creating technical documents for this project.

I created a User Manual to help the operators of the machine understand and use all the features provided by the software. Wrote a Production manual outlining the various processes and parts involved in the final assembly of the product and the time taken by each stage in the production chain. A Service manual containing instructions for the engineers to perform standard trouble shooting routines and to use Software Utility for fault diagnosis. Installation Guide that contains checklists for the engineer to cross check before the machine is powered on at any customer site. And an in-house technical document describing the function of each hardware block and the structure of the microcontroller program.

Figure 8.2: Crammed Resume

The former is crammed with information and the prospective employer will have to take efforts to and information in this type of resume. The format and layout of the latter is pleasing to the eyes. It is also easy to scan through the lists to locate the information and understand what it is about.

8.8 Highlight Activities and Skills

The main aim of your resume is to gain interviews for a particular position. So, ensure to cite the activities in order of their importance to that job.

Period: Aug 1997-98 (1 year)

Company: XYZ India Ltd.

Designation: Senior Development Engineer

Nature of Job: Development of Electronic Hardware for Computer Controlled Instruments/Systems.

The Automatic Compression Testing Machine is a computer controlled machine that is used in cement houses to measure the strength of concrete samples. The software provides a graphical interface to the operator of the machine with various options to conduct test runs, save test data, perform analysis on the saved data, manage data files and operator information.

Apart from developing the Electronic Hardware for this machine, I was also responsible for creating technical documents for this project:

- User Manual to help the operators of the machine understand and use all the features provided by the software.
- Production manual outlining the various processes and parts involved in the final assembly of the product and the time taken by each stage in the production chain.
- Service manual containing instructions for the engineers to perform standard trouble shooting routines and to use a Software Utility for fault diagnosis.
- Installation Guide that contains checklists for the engineer to cross check before the machine is powered on at any customer site.
- An in house technical document describing the function of each hardware block and the structure of the microcontroller program.

Figure 8.3 Organized and Structured Resume

If you are applying for the post of an administrative executive, ensure that:

- The objective is specific to the position.
- You have a list of appropriate skill sets.
- Experience if any is about administration related work profile.

Omit information that may seem important to you, but is unrelated and irrelevant to the position applied for. The less you say about your unrelated experience, the more impact the related activities will have.

8.9 Play the Matching Game

Review the job responsibilities and check for the key words listed in the advertisements you plan to respond to. When writing your resume, use those key words in your resume.

If your resume is already available, check if you have missed any key words, and add them to your resume.

Assume a job advertisement wherein the requirements are:

- BE/DME.
- 4 to 7 years of experience out of which at least 3 years are in forging industry.
- Knowledge of UNIGRAPHICS/CATIA/ANSYS.
- Experience on CAD modelling and CNC toolpath generation of forging components like cran-shafts, con-rod, knuckles is required.

In such a case, if you have the relevant skills and experience you should mention them up front. Here, Figure 8.4: A contains the important and relevant information, but B stands out better as it aptly maps out the requirement of the company in the three sections.

Education:
- MBA Marketing
- Diploma in Quality Assurance (ISO9000)
- B.E.

Skill Set:
- XMI, ASP, JavaScript, NET
- Java, C, C++, Python
- UNIGRAPHICS, ANSYS

Experience:
- Programming
- CAD modelling software

A: Avoid

Education:
- B.E. (Mechanical)
- Diploma in Quality Assurance (ISO9000)
- MBA Marketing

Skill Set:
- UNIGRAPHICS (Expert: 4 years)
- ANSYS (Expert: 3 years)
- CATIA (Beginner: 1 year)

Experience:
- CAd modelling software
- CNC forging components crankshaft, con-rod

B: Better

Figure 8.4: Matching Skills with Requirement

8.10 Include Quantitative Information

Quantitative information provides a sense of the size and scope of the positions and responsibilities held, and the real value of the stated achievements. You can include information that best defines the level and scope of that responsibility and achievement.

Example: Avoid: *Led projects.*

Better 1: *Led a project worth $1 million budget to completion.*

Better 2: *Led a project that got us $1 million worth business from XYZ.*

The phrase *led projects* sounds very generic and does not contain any information. Whereas the other two statements are not only very impressive, but also gives a generic idea about the project.

If you are applying for the position of a sales engineer, stating/ increased profits may not hold much value as it is your job profile and you are expected to do that. But mentioning that you have increased product sales by 45% (provided you have really achieved it), will give the hiring managers a good feel of your performance and achievement. Quantitative information, thus, improves the value of your resume.

8.11 Be Consistent

Ensure to follow rules of uniformity, consistency, and parallelism. Be consistent about:

- The styles and formats.
- Use of phrases.
- Formatting. Use of italics, capital letters, bullets, boldface, and underlining.
- The alignment of the text for different elements.
- Use of abbreviations and capitalizations.
- The use of font for a certain level of heading.

- The style of phrasing for similar information in a resume. For example, if you have written your skill-sets in Times font, all the skills should be in Times font. Having said this, ensure to use different font types with discretion, only to highlight the text.

8.12 Watch Your Verb Tense

The trend is to use the first person (I), though some people still use the third person (he, she). I personally don't like the latter because it gives a feeling that someone else has created the resume for you. Hence, the connection that the recruiter feels for you as an applicant will be lacking. But which ever you choose, use it consistently, with a tight watch over the verb tense.

- If the accomplishment is completed, use past tense.

  Example: *I have conducted more than 15 training sessions.*

- If the task is still underway, use present continuous tense.

  Example: *I am conducting training sessions on corporate communication.*

- If the skill has been used in the past and will continue to be used, use present tense.

  Example: *I conduct training sessions on corporate communication.*

8.13 Highlight Your Skills

Emphasize your technical skills and other strengths. Portray yourself in the best possible way. The resume should reflect all the skills you have.

- If you know a software package or if you have a scientific background, make sure you give the details.
- Even if you have just started learning something new, say CATIA, add it under the skill sets marking it as learning.

Try to mention all the skills required for the position you are applying for.

ANSYS	(Expert: 3 years)
CATIA	(Beginner: learning)
UNIX	(Beginner: learning)
Perl	(Expert: 5 years)
Java	(Expert: 3 years)

Play up all the qualities that qualify you the particular position. Highlight your breadth of knowledge. Mention every skill that demonstrates progress and/or accomplishments due directly to your work.

- Emphasize on the format. In Figure 8.2 the responsibilities handled in the previous organization is lost in the paragraph. Only a patient and/or desperate employer will try to read through and locate the information. Fewer employers may mark it for future reference.

8.14 Telephone Number That Will be Answered

If the hiring person consider you for an interview, they should be in a position to easily contact you without much effort from their part.

- Make certain your phone number and e-mail address are clearly visible in the resume. Do not make the interviewers search for it.
- Be sure to add a phone number on the resume that will be answered by a person or an answering machine. Do not lose the opportunity of an interview merely because there was no answer to the call made to you in spite of repeated calls.
- If you are not in a position to take calls during the working hours, it would be a good idea to mention it in your resume. If space permits, mention the reason why and indicate the duration when you could be available in the day time for a brief talk.

Example: *I work in a BPO and so, I won't be available for a telephonic talk from 8.30 am to 5.30 pm. But you may call me between 12.30 and 1.00 pm during my lunch time for a brief discussion.*

- If you are providing land line, ensure to include the area code. The recruiters may not have the time to try to find out the area code. It will be easier for them to check another resume instead of trying to figure out your area code.

8.15 Avoid Weird E-mail-IDs

Some candidates use crazy and weird sounding e-mail address such as crazygirl@yahoo.co.in, funkyboy@gmail.co.in, iamafreak@hotmail.com. There is nothing wrong in using such e-mail ids provided you use them when corresponding with your friends. These should not be used for professional work. Who would want to recruit candidates who call themselves crazy girl, or funky boy, or a freak?

Even when you are thinking of stepping into a profession, you should look like, sound like, and seem like a professional.

8.16 Don't Stretch the Truth

Make sure that you can back up what you claims you make in your resume. So, keep the claims within the range of your own integrity. There is nothing wrong in adding things in your resume so you communicate clearly who you are and what you can do best. But avoid adding false statements and information. It will only land you into problems. For details, see Chapter A, Fudging Resumes.

8.17 Create a Suitable Format

One of the most important part of the resume writing process, which is often overlooked is the format. Do not blindly copy a format or template that has caught your fancy.

It might have worked for someone else, but that does not mean it will work for you. Create a format that is suitable to your requirement—that will highlight your strengths, skills, education, and experiences.

Employers usually do not have enough time to read through each of your resume to determine if you have the skills they need. They make a quick judgement when glancing at your resume. If they see unrelated job titles or skills or do not find the information they are looking for, they might assume that you are not qualified for the job. For details, see Chapter 4.

8.18 Do What Works

Do not blindly follow the rules and/or guidelines. Pick and choose what is best for you.

Everyone freely gives advice on resume length and the most common advise is to restrict it to one or two pages. If you can keep the reader's undivided attention and interest, there is no harm if your resume runs into pages.

At the same time, it should create an interest and excitement in the prospective employers to make them call you for an interview. You can divert from this rule in the following situations:

- If you are an entry level writer and don't have a portfolio of your work to show off, write an essay on why you have applied for the job and how well you will fit in. You can add this to the end of the resume.
- If you are a freelancer or a consultant, include details such as a list of well known clients, a list of publications, skills, assignments, quotes from former clients about how fantastic you are, etc.

8.19 Don't be a Copy Cat

There are no hard and fast rules in writing a resume. Though there are many rules, guidelines, and tips, you may also decide how best to create your resume based on the advertisement, the nature of the job you are looking, and the organization you are approaching. Put in some effort when creating your resume. If you don't, it will force the recruiters to wonder whether you will put in effort to perform at work.

You can take a look at other resumes to determine what you have to write and how, but start your resume from scratch. Writing your own resume will give you a chance to express who you truly are. Most importantly, during the interview, you will be in a position to explain why you have written certain things and why you have not.

I have come across situations wherein I have received identical resumes. In one case, I came across three identical resumes (the only difference was in the name, address, contact number and the percentage of marks). At first I thought that the recruitment agency must have prepared it for them. During the telephonic interview, two of them stated that they had created the resume themselves and their friends had copied it from them.

The third said that he copied it from a friend since he was not sure how to go about creating one and he did not have enough time to think about it. In the process of mentioning how helpful his friend was, he mentioned the name of the friend from whom he copied the resume. Needless to say, I invited two of them for the interview—the one who actually created the resume and the one who copied it. For me what mattered was the former was helpful and latter was truthful.

8.20 Let The Employer Decide

Write a resume to inform not to impress or enforce yourself. Remember you will be tested for your skills and qualities. Perform well during the interview and let the prospective employer come to their own conclusion about their opinion about you.

- Avoid using generic statements that don't add value to your resume.

  Example: *Instead of saying you have excellent leadership qualities, give an instance of how you lead a team or describe any activities* *that shows off your leadership qualities and other potential.*

- Don't use high sounding words to highlight your strengths or to grab attention, specially if you don't have those attributes.

  Example: *Don't call yourself dynamic if you are meek and introvert. The reason is, during the period of the interview, you will come across as anything else, but dynamic. The interviewer will assume that either you are a liar or that you don't understand the language well.*

8.21 Don't Misdirect

Most of the resumes come to human resources department without any subject line. If there is one, the subject line may be *for any suitable post or Raju's Resume, or Resume for the available position, or Job application,* which does not make any sense to the person sorting the resumes. They are forced to read the mail to understand for which position the person has applied for and then move the resume (or the email) to the respective folder. Most of the time, such e-mails may go unnoticed.

Avoid	Better
• For any suitable post	• Resume: Design Engineer
• Raju's Resume	• Resume: Software Engineer (Raju)
• Job application	• Job application: Trainee Engineer
• Resume for available position	• Resume: HR Executive
• My resume	• Resume: Sr. Engineer (5 years exp)

This actually shows that the candidate is not focussed in thought. As a prospective candidate, write professional cover letter to make the connection to the job you are applying for. Also ensure to write a reasonable subject line.

8.22 Electronic Resumes

In the early 90s, people rarely thought of submitting resumes online. Today, things have changed. The internet is one of the fastest ways to get your information to an employer, but to do so you will need a resume that can either be send by e-mail or uploaded onto a job seeking site. There are two types of electronic resumes: e-mail resumes and scannable resumes.

- **E-mail resume:** It is one that will be sent as the body of the e-mail. It must be written in plain text without excess text formatting. That is, avoid using bold, italics, underlining, and bullet as they don't translate well in most e-mail programs. Also avoid using tabs.

  These days, attachments (in PDF and MS Word format) are also used.

- **Scannable resume:** A scannable resume is formatted for easy scanning into a computer for storage in a searchable database. To facilitate scanning, avoid bold, italics, bullets, or underlining, and use a common font like Courier or Times New Roman. If your resume will be scanned into a database, it is also important to use appropriate keywords.

8.23 Error Free

Spelling or typographical errors, grammatical weaknesses and unusual punctuation stand out like a sore thumb. The resume should be neat and error free.

- Education: Graduation, August *1896*-May 1999
- *Develop* and recommend an annual operating expense *fudget*.
- I am a *rabid* typist
- Instrumental ion *ruining* entire operation for a Midwest chaiin operation

This is not joke, but the type of typos you come across in the resumes. Edit and proof read your resume that your resume is free of errors.

- Proof read the resume to catch any hidden mistakes.
- Check for grammar and punctuation.
- Perform a spell check.
- Ensure that you have used consistent font types, syntax, and capitalization.

After doing all you these, fine-tune your resume. If you feel that your skills need emphasis using bold or italic, go ahead and do it, but don't over do anything.

8.24 Review Your Resumes

It goes unsaid that you have to check and recheck your resume before you send it. Review it for content, usability, and error. It is also a good idea to have someone else review your resume. In your attempt to show off your accomplishments you may not be showing off all your skills and positive points clearly.

1. Discuss with someone about your job objective.
2. Show the person the listings of positions that interest you
3. Ask the person to review your cover letter and your resume.
4. Encourage them to ask questions. Their questions can help you to discover items you inadvertently left off your resume.
5. Revise your resume to include these items. Their questions can also point to items on your resume that are confusing to the reader.
6. Clarify your resume based on this input.

8.25 The Golden Rule

There may be many guidelines and tips for creating a good resume, but there is only one golden rule. That is to sell the product—YOU. You need to sell yourself like you are the best thing on the planet. Bad sales people are quite, meek, submissive, negative, and desperate. On the other hand, good sales people are:

- Positive.
- Enthusiastic.
- Assertive, but not aggressive.
- Honest. They do not volunteer wrong information.

Chapter 9 Fudging Resumes

Making some unrealistic changes and additions to the information in your resume may seem like a good idea. In fact, you may feel that it is harmless. You probably think that a little white lie will never hurt anyone. It can be especially tempting when you are without a job and are searching for one for months. However, we all know that lies in any form is not a good idea.

As the saying goes, you will have to lie to hide one lie. The process will just go on till the situation gets messy. So, it is best not to lie. The saying: "*A half a truth is a whole lie*" is applicable here. This chapter discusses the following topics:

- ❒ **Section 9.1:** What Is Fudging?
- ❒ **Section 9.2:** Why People Fudge?
- ❒ **Section 9.3:** What People Lie About?
- ❒ **Section 9.4:** Known Examples
- ❒ **Section 9.5:** Avoid Fudging

9.1 What Is Fudging?

Fudging means to include or alter some information regarding employment history, education, salary, or designation in your resume. Anything as small as (so you may think) the following activities comes under fudging:

- Stretching the duration of employment (even by a few months).
- Enhancing your title to make it appear a little more important.
- Using misleading words like "implemented" instead of "participated".
- Mentioning that you have a certification if you have only attended the class without appearing for the exam.
- Changing the duties and responsibilities you have handled.
- Stating that you have resigned when you were actually asked to leave due to low performance or laid-off due to unknown reasons.

In short, fudging is about faking information in the resume to deceive the human resources person or hiring managers in order to get hired. The most common resume fabrications involve reasons for:

- **Leaving a previous job**
- **Claims about accomplishments**
- **Job responsibilities**
- **Designation**
- **Compensation and benefits**
- **Salary**
- **Scope of duties**
- **Education**

Job applicants often embellish their credentials to give themselves an added advantage in the fiercely competitive job market. This may also mean that after faking in the resume, the supporting documents included with the resume like, the experience, salary information, experience, and references are also changed or fabricated.

Unfortunately, people barely think about the implications of falsifying the information, probably because as far as they are concerned, what they are doing are very minor alterations. It can also be called *fibbing, fabricating, faking*. Believe it or not, you can also call it *doctoring* a resume.

9.2 Why People Fudge?

The persons tampering with their resumes are probably desperate to get a job (or another job). Most of the time people tamper with their resume in the following cases:

- When they are offered from their job for non-performance.
- When they are laid-off.
- Have major hiccups in their professional life.
- Handle more and higher responsibilities with lower job title (so might change their designation). For details, see Section 9.3.1, Designations/Titles.
- Have employment gaps that have no valid explanations.
- Not really good at what they do.
- Desperate to impress the potential hiring managers.
- Do not have the required skills or relevant experience.
- Lack of relevant job opportunity in the market.
- Non-availability of progress path in existing organizations because of lack of performance or lack of self-motivation.

9.2.1 No Valid Experience

When looking for a change in career, you may not have the valid experience or relevant skills. Since it is a change in career, the interviewers will know that you have certain limitations. So actually, there is absolutely no need to lie on your resume.

Example: *Ketki was an engineer, working in* ***Company 1*** *as a content developer. Over a period of time, she developed some interest in software testing. She applied to a couple of advertisements for the position of QA engineer. To make her experience look worthwhile, she added product QA and product testing and some of her secondary set of responsibilities to the list.*

Ketki worked in ***Company 2*** *as a software testing engineer (they did not have the concept of a trainee). After a year, Ketki decided to move on and soon joined* ***Company 3****. In her resume she mentioned that her designation in* ***Company 1*** *was trainee software testing engineer and her experience was primarily in software testing. Content development was an extra responsibility she performed, because she was good at it.*

Based on her experience in ***Company 2****, she did reasonably well in her interview and soon joined* ***Company 3*** *as a senior QA specialist. Unfortunately, one of her colleagues from* ***Company 1****, working in another department, attended an interview in* ***Company 3****. When the HR spoke to the candidate about Ketki, he innocently mentioned that he knew a Ketki who worked as a content developer.*

Ketki's little secret was out. Unfortunately, Ketki did not think that she did anything wrong, after all, it was a minor alteration. She argued her point. After a lot of deliberation, Ketki was fired.

9.2.2 Not Good Performers

Many a times, people with some experience, but having the *need to improve* discussions with their bosses or supervisors will want to check greener pastures instead of taking the advice and making some improvements. Such people might lie about the specific areas.

Chances are, the emphasis of strengths will be in the areas they lack in.

- Don't write *hard working,* if you are *hardly working.*
- If you were a member of the team when certain process was being implemented, don't write that you implemented the process.

The hiring managers can pick on such lies during the interview. Even if they don't, they soon will after you start working for them.

9.2.3 Insecurity

One of the main reasons of fudging is insecurity. Most of the time people forge their resume because they don't have a job. They are simply desperate and insecure.

Some lies don't appear on a resume but are verbally crafted. There have been a number of cases in recent years where executives or coaches have lied about military service, trying to use their experience to motivate employees or athletes.

Example: *Former Toronto Blue Jays manager Tim Johnson concocted a story about serving in battle in Vietnam, which proved unlikely for someone who spent the war stateside in the Reserves. He was eventually offered by the club.*

9.2.4 Request for Change

Sometimes you may be requested by the recruiting companies to make some changes so that it will be easier for them to match you to the right job or the *vice versa.* In any case, the arrangement is beneficial to them.

But remember that the ethical responsibility for a true representation of your skills, achievements, and experience lies directly with you. You are the person being hired and you are the person making the claims. You will be the one in trouble at a later stage. So, don't entertain such requests.

Note: *I am not suggesting that all the recruiting companies come up with such requests. Some are very professional to the core.*

9.2.5 HR Policies

Most of the time, the HR related matters are so diverse across industries and even in similar departments.

- In some organizations, designations are very liberal. They are very catchy and tempting, but not actually suitable for the years of experience or skills the person might have. After 2-3 years of experience, the employee gets the job title of team leader or project manager.
- Some organizations are very strict in their designations. People with no experience are initially taken in as trainees. They become team leader after 7-8 years of valid experience, only if they show leadership qualities.

Sometimes I am forced to think that unhealthy HR policies is also one of the major reasons that make people fudge or pad their resumes as far as designation or job profile are considered. During the initial stages of the recruiting process, the HR usually shortlist resumes on the basis of keywords like experience, software tools, qualification, educational institutes, location, current salary, etc.

They probably give more importance to higher degrees or extra certification than skills. Candidates might miss a chance to get shortlisted just because their resume may not have such keywords or information. Often, this makes the applicants fudge or pad up their resumes a bit.

9.3 What People Lie About?

You need to understand that you need not lie about anything if the resume is well-written, strategically organized, and emphasises on the appropriate skills. You may explain to the interviewers any employment gaps and point out to the fact that you have shown the time gap in your resume. This will show off your honesty and integrity.

The most common misleading information put on resumes are:

- Higher titles/designations
- Inaccurate employment dates. It is usually done to cover up:
  - — Gaps in employment
  - — Frequent job hopping
  - — Irrelevant jobs
  - — Sort stint in an organization
- Half-finished degrees
- Higher education
- Inflated salaries
- Accomplishments
- Roles, duties, responsibilities held at the job

9.3.1 Designations/Titles

Do not try to impress the potential hiring managers by using the job titles you never had. You may be tempted to use them because of the following reasons:

- You perform the duties of the suggested title.
- You have a lesser known title.
- You assume that you know the details about job function of a certain designation.
- You have less responsibilities with higher job title.

Perform the Duties of the Suggested Title

Perhaps your current job title does not properly convey all the duties or responsibilities that you are handling. Even though you are performing many of the duties the title suggests, avoid using titles or designation you don't actually hold.

Example: *You may want to show your designation as a manager where as you have worked as a* ***team leader****, performing all the duties of a manager (or so you think). If you are not a manager, don't call yourself one just because you are handling some of the duties of a manager.*

During the interview, you can describe the responsibilities and duties you handle. Remember, the abilities and skills of a manager are much more than that is visible to you. You may think that you have it all, but the recruiters are intelligent enough to make up their mind about your abilities.

Seniority also means being capable of making the right and well-thought about decisions regarding projects and people. You should not only know about the job responsibilities and about the departmental processes but should also be in a position to take the important decisions that a project manager is capable of doing.

Have a Lesser Known Title

Your organization may not follow the market norms and uses lesser known designation that probably only your organization uses. In such a situation, you may go ahead and use a commonly used title.

Example: *Consider a situation where in you have two years experience and are working as a web developer performing all the activities involved in web development. If your designation is* ***production specialist,*** *you may call yourself as a* ***web developer,*** *but definitely not a* ***senior web developer.***

As far as possible, use the designation that you currently have. Change titles only if your existing title does not clarify your position and is confusing. Even in such cases, it is better to be honest.

Example: Avoid: *Web developer*

Better: *Production Specialist (equivalent to "Web developer" in the market*

You Think Know the Details

If you are a senior engineer and know about the duties of a project manager, don't call yourself as one just because you are aware about the job responsibilities.

- Bookish knowledge and what you think you have seen and understood is very different from the knowledge you gain from actual experience.
- You may think that you know all that is essential and required for the next level. But think that you know and actually knowing the requirements are different aspects altogether. The employers will determine your level of responsibility based upon your knowledge and experience.

Higher Job Title

You may be handling very limited and lesser responsibilities with higher job title. This happens when organizations give away titles like: senior engineer, project manager, or team leader to a person having 2-3 years experience. In such a scenario, you may not be aware of all the related responsibilities for that position. So, the tendency is to add up more roles and responsibilities specific to the designation they have.

9.3.2 Experience

Receiving good ratings or remarks at your current organization, does not mean that you know everything about your job. Many a times you may think that you do, but the truth could be that you actually don't!

If you are interviewing for a senior position, you will be asked questions about the projects, accomplishments, and responsibilities that you held. Most of the candidates with about 3-4 years experience tell how quality conscious and productive they are.

After the training period, you are expected to be productive and produce quality work. So, after 3-4 years, being productive or quality conscious are certainly not major accomplishments.

Seniority brings in credibility and you will have to prove to the interviewers how you added value to a certain project. In such a situation, you need to have in-depth knowledge of the department, processes, the project you handle, and the decisions you take. If you are vague in your answers and lack any details in your management experience, you are sure to rise suspicions.

You need not fake about your abilities in your resume. If you are capable and have the appropriate skills and aptitude for the position you have applied for, you can prove it during the interview. The interviewers will opt for you over a more experienced person because even with lesser level of experience, you are probably far more capable than an experienced and senior candidate. So, if you are applying for a senior position in another organization, don't lie about:

- The duration of work experience.
- The skills you possess.
- The job responsibilities you handle.

9.3.3 Employment Gaps

These days employment gap is not a matter of stigma or embarrassment. Losing a job due to down-sizing or lay-offs has less stigma attached to it. But still, employers are a little extra vary when considering such candidates. The credibility and performance of such candidates are sometimes questioned.

- If you were out of work for about a year during which time you took courses to enhance your education or professional credentials, list this under the academic section on your resume. This is much better than pretending the period of unemployment never happened.
- Most of the employers are now sympathetic to time taken by women for personal and family reasons, specially after

child birth. They understand that people, specially woman have their priorities and respect such decisions.

Instead of fudging the dates of your previous jobs to cover an employment gap, address the reason of the gap in the cover letter. If you are laid-off mention it. Many recruiters appreciate and admire honesty.

9.3.4 Employment Period

Most of time people may add a few months, or a year, or a couple of years to the employment period to pad it up.

- People may add a few months either way — to the earlier job or the later job if they have held a job for a few months in between.

Example: *Shilpa worked in* ***Company 1*** *from May 1998 till February 2001, in* ***Company 2*** *from March 2001 till June 2001, and in* ***Company 3*** *from June 2001 till July 2003.*

She did not want to show the three and a half months experience in ***Company 2*** *as it would go against her. So, she added two months to the earlier job in* ***Company 1*** *and made it from May 1998 till April 2001. She added the rest to the later job in* ***Company 3*** *and made it from May 2001 till July 2006.*

Shilpa did not think that she was doing anything wrong as she just added a couple of months to an existing larger experience–two months along with 2 years and 10 months and 1.5 months with 2 years. Unfortunately, this comes across as lying about your employment period.

- People may add a year or a couple of years if they were either without a job or held a couple of jobs of shorter duration in between.

Example: *Ratna worked in* ***Company 1*** *for six years, from Jan. 1995 till Dec. 2000. Then, she* *worked in 4 other places during the period of 1.5 years.*

When Ratna applied for her next job, her resume showed that she worked for ***Company 1*** *from Jan. 1995 till Dec. 2001 (i.e., for 7 years). She then showed a break of six months where she mentioned that she did a course with some organization but did not appear for the exam.*

Needless to say, her lie about the period of experience and certification course was caught about 7 months after she joined the new organization. Though she was not asked to leave, she lost her credibility.

- Some people write vague dates which allows the reader to misinterpret the information. Dates of employment are designed to cover up gaps in employment.

Example: *Sonal mentioned in her resume that she worked in an organization from 2007 to 2008, creating the impression that she worked there for almost an year. In fact, she worked there only 4 months—from October 2007 to January 2008.*

As far as possible avoid misrepresentation of information. Be very specific in your resume. Don't give a scope to the interviewer to hold anything against you.

9.3.5 Degree

There may be cases where in candidates missed out obtaining the bachelors or masters certification inspite of having attended the course. Chances are that they could not give the examination or missed just one paper, but could not follow it up and complete it.

- Half-finished degrees should not be listed in the educational qualification list. Even if you have almost completed your degree (that is attended all the classes, but did not appear for the exam), you cannot list it as a completed degree on your resume. If you have not completed a higher degree do not try to fudge it.

- No education is ever wasted. So, you can give yourself that credit and mention a note that you have attended the XYZ course, but did not complete it.

Dec 2007:	Certification in Software Testing *(Did not appear for the final exam)*
Feb 2006:	Certification in Technical Writing
Jun 2005:	M.Sc. Physics
Mar 2003:	Certification in Software Programing
Jun 2002:	B.Sc. Physics
Jun 1999:	HSC (12th)
Jun 1997:	SSC (10th)

- You may also indicate if you plan to complete the degree and by when you plan to do it. This will also show your truthfulness and honesty.

9.4 Known Examples

There has been many high profile cases of fudging. The latest and the very Indian case is about Varun Gandhi. On March 19, 2009, Varun Gandhi appealed to the Allahabad High Court to clear himself off the criminal case filed against him for making hate speeches in Pilibhit. In his petition, he claimed to have graduated from the London School of Economics (LSE), and then received a Masters degree at the School of Oriental and African Studies (SOAS).

Both LSE and SOAS have now said his claim is not accurate. Zeba Salman, alumni relations officer at SOAS, said Varun Gandhi did not complete his course at SOAS.

"Feroze Varun Gandhi withdrew from his M.Sc. programe at SOAS, and hence did not actually graduate from SOAS."

Can you tell what do the following people have in common?

- Jeffrey Papows, the chairman of Lotus, a subsidiary of IBM.
- George O'Leary, the head football coach at Notre Dame.
- Sandra Baldwin, the president of the United States Olympic Committee.
- Kenneth Lonchar, the chief financial officer of Veritas.
- Ronald Zarella, the CEO of Bausch Lomb.
- David Edmondson, the chief executive officer of RadioShack.
- Joseph John Ellis, the Professor of History at the Mount Holyoke College.
- Quincy Troupe, the poet laureate for the State of California.

All of them lied on their resumes and as a result lost their jobs, except for Ronald Zarella. Bausch Lomb CEO Ronald Zarella lied about having an MBA for ten years. The lie was revealed in 2002. Fortunately for Zarella, the company kept him.

- In 2000, Jeffrey Papows, chairman of Lotus, a subsidiary of IBM had to resign because he made up facts about his life, including a Ph.D. and a black belt.
- In 2001, George O'Leary included a masters degree he did not have and letters for playing football that he never earned on his resume. He did this because he wanted the job in collegiate sports head coach of Notre Dame football.
- In 2002, Sandra Baldwin, the first woman president of the United States Olympic Committee, resigned after it was revealed that she had lied about having a Ph.D. in English from Arizona State University.
- In 2002, Kenneth Lonchar the chief financial officer and executive vice president of Veritas Software resigned after the company learned he falsified his educational credentials, including an MBA from Stanford. *Ironically, in Latin, **veritas** means **truth**.*

- In 2006, David J. Edmondson, the chief executive of RadioShack, was fired after a newspaper investigation showed that his resume included two degrees in psychology and theology, degrees he never got from a university that was not even accredited.

- Joseph John Ellis is a Pulitzer Prize-winning Professor of History on the Ford Foundation at Mount Holyoke College. He is the former dean of faculty at Mount Holyoke and also served as Acting President for part of 1984 while President Elizabeth Topham Kennan was on leave.

  According to the Wikipedia (http://en.wikipedia.org/wiki/Joseph J. Ellis), Ellis became the subject of controversy when the Boston Globe published an article on June 18, 2001, revealing that he had exaggerated his involvement in the Vietnam War. He served in uniform in America but did not go to Vietnam as he had claimed to students and to the media. Ellis acknowledged the mistake and issued a public apology. Mount Holyoke suspended him from both his endowed chair as well as from teaching during the 2001-2002 academic year. His accomplishments are real, motivating, and impressive. So, we do not know why Joseph J. Ellis fabricated his past when he had no need to do it.

9.5 Avoid Fudging

In June 2008, Tata Consultancy Service (TCS), asked 20 employees at its Kolkata centre to leave. During the background verification, it was found that these employees have used fudged resumes to get jobs. TCS is not the only firm who has taken this process very seriously. Infosys and Wipro are also known to take strict action.

- If you take a risk of lying to get into one organization, chances are during the cross-check the HR may find out the information provided by you is incorrect.

  Unlike years ago, employers today conduct extensive background checks. Chances are that prospective employer will gather a great deal of other personal information about you. In many cases, it is not unusual for large companies to hire outside firms to conduct the evaluation.

- Human resources and department managers usually have a wide professional network outside the organization. They talk about, discuss, and cross check information about the candidates.
- You not only loose your opportunity in the place you applied for, but in the future you may not be in a position to get a job in other organizations because they may have already heard a lot about you.
- To hide a lie, you will have to tell another. In the process, to hide a couple of lies, you will tell a few more. The process just goes on till the situation gets out of your control and gets messy.
- If you are really not a good performer, the major problem is that once you land up with the job, your employer will discover quickly that you are not as *qualified*, or *skilled*, *experienced* as you claimed.
- More employers are taking the time to check facts, such as dates of employment, degrees held, responsibilities handled at a previous organization, etc.
- Sometimes what started off as a harmless lie will put you in a very tight position. In spite of being a good performer, people will be upset by the fact that you lied to them.

Lay-offs and down-sizing is not a new phenomenon. Losing a job to down-sizing or lay-offs, specially if it is done in large numbers, has less stigma attached to it because it does not happen just because of bad performance. These days, many employers are more sympathetic to time off taken for personal and family reasons and consider candidates who are eligible for the required position.

Gaps in employment, both short-term and long-term, can now be more easily explained than in the past. So, think twice before you decide to embellish your resume.

Appendix A

Resume Questions

As a job seeker you are probably so involved in searching your own requirements and interest, so much so that it may become hard to take a step back and write a marketable resume. Use all the information you have read about creating a workable and attractive resume.

- Think of your resume as a marketing tool.
- Think of yourself as a product, potential employers as your customers, and your resume as a brochure about you.
- Market yourself through your resume.
- Highlight all the positive aspects of your skills and strengths.
- Mention what makes you unique and different from the others.

If you have ever attempted to write your own resume you know how difficult it is to write about yourself objectively. If you are a good self-critic and can truly review yourself, you can make things easier. A successful person is the one who is able to do a proper self-analysis. To be successful in life you should be able to identify your shortcomings and your strengths without any issues or egos. If you are able to do it, you can develop your strengths and work on your shortcomings.

To make the resume writing process easier, answer a few questions truthfully. Use the answers to create your resumes and highlight your skills using appropriate action verbs.

- What is it that your boss or supervisor always depends on you? [*quality, completing work on time, tools, troubleshooting, etc.*]
- According to your team members what you are especially good at? [*technology, troubleshooting, etc.*]
- Have you ever gone above and beyond your job description? [*mentoring, peerchecks, creating newsletter, etc.*]
- What do you know so well that you could teach it to others?
- What skills are you good at? [*programing, training, communication, writing, etc.*]
- What are your competitive strengths?
  - If your friends at work were to describe your strengths, what would they say?
  - If your foes at work were to describe your strengths, what would they say?
  - If you have to describe your strengths yourself, what would you brag about?
- For each position you held, list about two achievements. [***Engineer:*** *mentored, set process.* ***Sr. Engineer:*** *mentored, conducted training*]

- What improvement have you provided the department since you joined their team? [*set quality processes, created scripts to automate the work*]
- Have you been involved in designing and/or implementing new initiatives?
- Have you conducted a training session? What do people feel about you? [*good trainer, good presenter, interesting and interactive sessions*]
- Is the management proud of you? Why? [*started in-house training for better writing, communication skills, and C++*]
- What difficulties or barriers have you overcome to get to the position you are now?
- What creative activities have you done that you feel proud about? [*in-house training, internal newsletter, co-ordinated events, etc.*]
- Describe something you designed and created that you are happy about? [*web page, format of a document, newsletter, advertisement layout, etc.*]
- Describe something you made or fixed up, that gave you a strong sense of satisfaction. [*started training sessions, updated guidelines, automated scripts, etc.*]
- What praise or acknowledgement did you get from your employers for a job well done?
- Has there any *problem* that no one was able to solve, but you did it with *conviction*? [*worked on creating the functionality of the software no one was ready to work on*]
- What praise or *award* did you get from a customer for a problem you solved so effortlessly?
- Name 3-5 *qualities* or characteristics of each of your team member that you most respect or admire the most.

- What do people say about your abilities? [*dependable, productive, etc.*]
- If you are on vacation, do your work team members miss your presence? [*probably yes, but you need to ask them this question*]
- If you are away for a day or two, will the team members will able to continue their work with out any hindrance?
- If you are away for a few days, will the team members will happy about your absence? Will it be *when the cat is away, the mice will play situation*?

These are some pointers that will help you start thinking in the correct direction. You can think of more questions and add them to this list.

Appendix B Action Verbs

You have created your resume. But don't forget to check if it seems to be alive and lively. A lifeless, dead resume will not ignite the spark of interest in the interviewers. So, what do you do? Try to give life and activate your resume with some action-oriented words.

- Action words or verbs ignite and give life to the otherwise dull resume.
- They give your credentials a certain amount to authority and power. Hence, they are also called the *power words.*
- They capture the attention of hiring managers.

These words are considered important as they show the hiring managers what actions you have taken in previous jobs or what skills you possess. Finding the right verbs for your resume is also the key to standing out above the competition and getting a job interview.

It is easy to find the right verbs to make a great resume. If you have applied to several jobs of the same type, you may notice the same verbs are repeatedly requested in the job descriptions.

A word of caution though, using too many verbs can lead to buzzword overkill. That is, it may be harmful, rather than help your chances of getting a job interview. No hiring manager likes a resume saturated with lots of action words. It may sound fabricated. So choose your action verbs with care.

1. Depending on the job description and your experience, identify the actions employers value.
2. Match them to your qualifications, experience, and accomplishments.
3. Precede your skills and accomplishments with the appropriate action word.
4. End each statement with concise facts and figures.
5. Read the resume to check if you have used appropriate action words:
   - If they are very less, add some more.
   - If the resume is too saturated with action verbs, remove some.

B.1 Generic Keywords

accelerated	accomplished	accounted for
achieved	acted	activated
acquired	adapted	added
addressed	adjusted	administered
advanced	advised	advocated
aided	allocated	analyzed

answered	anticipated	applied
appointed	appraised	approved
arbitrated	arranged	ascertained
assembled	assessed	assigned
assisted	assumed	assured
attained	attended	audited
augmented	authored	authorized
awarded	balanced	began
boosted	bought	briefed
brought	budgeted	built
calculated	captured	catalogued
caught	chaired	changed
checked	chose	clarified
classified	cleared up	closed
coached	collaborated	collected
combined	communicated	compared
completed	composed	computed
conceived	conceptualized	concluded
condensed	conditioned	conducted
conferred	conserved	consolidated
constructed	consulted	continued
contributed	controlled	convinced
co-ordinated	corrected	corresponded
counselled	crafted	created
critiqued	cultivated	customized
dealt	debated	debugged
decided	defined	delegated
delivered	demonstrated	designated
designed	detected	determined
developed	devised	diagnosed
digested	directed	discovered
displayed	distributed	documented
diverted	documented	drafted
dramatized	drew	dropped
drove	earned	edited

educated	effected	elected
eliminated	employed	encouraged
enforced	engineered	enhanced
enlarged	enlisted	ensured
entered	entertained	established
estimated	evaluated	examined
excelled	executed	exercised
expanded	expedited	experimented
explained	explored	expressed
extended	extracted	facilitated
fabricated	facilitated	familiarized
fashioned	figured	filed
financed	fixed	followed
forecasted	formed	formulated
forwarded	fostered	found
founded	fulfilled	furnished
gained	gathered	generated
governed	graded	grossed
guided	handled	hastened
headed	heightened	helped
hiked	hired	honed
hosted	housed	hunted
identified	illustrated	imagined
implemented	improved	improvised
included	incorporated	increased
indexed	indicated	influenced
informed	initiated	innovated
inspected	inspired	installed
instituted	instructed	insured
integrated	interacted	interpreted
interviewed	introduced	invented
inventoried	investigated	involved
joined	judged	kept
laboured	launched	learned
lectured	led	licensed

lifted	listened	located
logged	made	maintained
managed	manipulated	mapped out
marketed	maximized	measured
mediated	merged	mentored
mobilized	modelled	modified
monitored	motivated	moved
navigated	negotiated	netted
observed	obtained	offered
operated	ordered	organized
originated	outlined	overcame
overhauled	oversaw	paid
painted	participated	perceived
performed	persevered	persuaded
photographed	piloted	pinpointed
pioneered	placed	planned
played	predicted	prepared
presented	prescribed	presided
prevented	prevailed	printed
prioritized	processed	produced
profited	programmed	projected
promoted	proofread	proposed
protected	proved	provided
publicized	purchased	qualified
questioned	raised	ran
rated	reached	read
realized	reasoned	received
recognized	recommended	reconciled
recorded	recruited	redesigned
reduced	referred	regulated
related	remodelled	rendered
renovated	reorganized	repaired
replaced	reported	represented
rescued	researched	resolved
responded	resulted in	restored

returned	retrieved	revealed
reviewed	revised	routed
saved	saw to it	scheduled
screened	scrutinized	searched
secured	selected	separated
served	serviced	shaped
shared	shipped	shored up
showed	sifted	simplified
simulated	sketched	smoothed
sold	solved	sorted
sought	specialized	specified
spoke	sponsored	standardized
started	straightened	streamlined
strengthened	structured	studied
submitted	suggested	summarized
supervised	supplied	supported
surpassed	surveyed	sustained
systematized	targeted	taught
terminated	tested	tightened
took	totalled	toured
tracked	trained	transcribed
transferred	transformed	transmitted
translated	travelled	treated
troubleshot	tutored	typed
uncovered	undertook	unearthed
unfurled	unified	united
updated	upgraded	used
utilized	validated	verbalized
verified	vitalized	volunteered
weighed	widened	welcomed
won	worked	wrote

B.2 Management/Leadership Skills

Administered	Analyzed	Appointed
Approved	Assigned	Attained

Authorized	Chaired	Considered
Consolidated	Contracted	Controlled
Co-ordinated	Decided	Delegated
Developed	Directed	Eliminated
Emphasized	Enforced	Enhanced
Established	Executed	Generated
Handled	Headed	Hired
Hosted	Improved	Incorporated
Increased	Initiated	Inspected
Led	Managed	Motivated
Organized	Over saw	Planned
Presided	Prioritized	Produced
Recommended	Reorganized	Replaced
Restored	Reviewed	Scheduled
Secured	Selected	Streamlined
Strengthened	Supervised	Terminated

B.3 Communication Skills

Addressed	Advertised	Arbitrated
Arranged	Articulated	Authored
Clarified	Collaborated	Communicated
Composed	Condensed	Conferred
Consulted	Contacted	Conveyed
Convinced	Corresponded	Debated
Defined	Developed	Directed
Discussed	Drafted	Edited
Enlisted	Explained	Expressed
Formulated	Furnished	Incorporated
Influence	Interacted	Interpreted
Interviewed	Involved	Joined
Judged	Lectured	Listened
Mediated	Moderated	Negotiated
Observed	Participated	Persuaded
Presented	Promoted	Proposed
Publicized	Reconciled	Recruited

Referred	Reinforced	Reported
Resolved	Responded	Specified
Spoke	Suggested	Summarized
Synthesized	Translated	Wrote

B.4 People Skills

Adapted	Advocated	Aided
Answered	Assessed	Assisted
Clarified	Coached	Collaborated
Contributed	Co-operated	Counselled
Demonstrated	Encouraged	Ensured
Expedited	Facilitated	Familiarized
Furthered	Guided	Helped
Motivated	Prevented	Provided
Referred	Represented	Resolved
Simplified	Supported	Volunteered

B.5 Technical Skills

Adapted	Applied	Assembled
Built	Calculated	Computed
Constructed	Converted	Debugged
Designed	Determined	Developed
Engineered	Fabricated	Fortified
Installed	Maintained	Operated
Overhauled	Programmed	Rectified
Regulated	Remodelled	Repaired
Replaced	Restored	Solved
Specialized	Standardized	Utilized

B.6 Organizational Skills

Arranged	Categorized	Classified
Coded	Collected	Compiled
Corrected	Corresponded	Distributed
Executed	Filed	Generated

Incorporated	Inspected	Logged
Maintained	Monitored	Obtained
Operated	Ordered	Organized
Prepared	Processed	Provided
Purchased	Recorded	Registered
Responded	Reviewed	Routed
Scheduled	Screened	Submitted
Supplied	Standardized	Systematized
Updated	Validated	Verified

B.7 Financial Skills

Administered	Adjusted	Allocated
Analyzed	Appraised	Assessed
Audited	Balanced	Budgeted
Calculated	Computed	Corrected
Determined	Developed	Estimated
Forecasted	Managed	Measured
Planned	Prepared	Programed
Projected	Qualified	Reconciled
Reduced	Researched	Retrieved

B.8 Research Skills

Analyzed	Clarified	Collected
Compared	Conducted	Critiqued
Detected	Determined	Diagnosed
Evaluated	Examined	Experimented
Explored	Formulated	Gathered
Inspected	Interviewed	Invented
Investigated	Located	Measured
Researched	Reviewed	Searched
Solved	Surveyed	Tested

B.9 Mentoring Skills

Adapted	Advised	Clarified
Coached	Communicated	Conducted
Co-ordinated	Critiqued	Developed
Enabled	Encouraged	Evaluated
Explained	Facilitated	Focused
Guided	Instilled	Instructed
Motivated	Persuaded	Simulated
Stimulated	Taught	Tested
Trained	Transmitted	Tutored

B.10 Creative Skills

Acted	Adapted	Combined
Composed	Conceptualized	Condensed
Created	Customized	Designed
Developed	Directed	Displayed
Entertained	Established	Fashioned
Formulated	Founded	Illustrated
Initiated	Instituted	Integrated
Introduced	Invented	Modelled
Modified	Originated	Performed
Photographed	Planned	Revised
Revitalized	Shaped	Solved

Appendix C Quick Summary

Creating an effective and usable resume is difficult, but not as difficult as you may think it to be. You just need to be focused, know your options, write well, and follow certain guidelines. When looking for a job, it is important to project a professional image of yourself.

The potential employer wants a neat, concise and focused presentation of your skills and experience to show him/her that you are well qualified to do the job he/she wants to accomplish. Your resume should be fat with facts from the top down, but this does not mean that you have to crowd your resume with everything you can think to say about yourself.

- There are no hard, set fast rules of resume writing. How you format the resume and what you would like to communicate is up to you. While there is wide agreement among the experts on many points about resume writing, the style, content, and format are dictated by what you want to communicate.
- Depending on the job search strategies you adopt, you may want two or three different resumes.
- Write and design your resume to sell you.
- The resume should be written to serve the purpose.
- A good format and organization guides the eye to keywords and speaks about the needs of the employer.
- Feel free to bold, underline, and italicize key portions that you would like to emphasize. But don't overdo it.
- Remember italics or wierd fonts that may be difficult to read.
- It should be visually pleasing.
- Create a good first impression and reflect your uniqueness.
- Revise and update your resume as your job search proceeds.
- Fous on readability. Remember that your resume may be scanned by the prospective employer for only 20-30 seconds.
- Organize the information in a logical manner.
- Ensure that your skills and experience match the requirment.
- Include quantitative information.
- Your resume never get you a job, but it will get you an interview. An interview is an opportunity to prove yourself and get the job. Don't lose you the opportunity of allowing the employer take a closer look at you.
- It should be fat with facts from the top down.

- Use an e-mail address that sounds professional. Avoid wierd email-Ids.
- Don't lie or fudge the resume.
- Add telephone numbers that will be answered by you or someone else.
- Resume is an outline of your achievement.
  - — Use short, concise phrases.
  - — Eliminate adjectives and adverbs.
  - — Ensure that each phrase clearly communicates a point.
  - — Keep it clutter free.
- It should attract attention to your special abilities and personal qualities.
- Include your employment dates.
- Use POWER words as it is a highly effective technique for highlighting skills.
- Use the present tense when describing current work; otherwise use past tense.
- Be sure your resume is error free. Many times resumes may not be given full consideration when there are typos and misinformation.
- Have several people critique your resume|ask your parents, a professor or a professional in your area of interest. They may catch something that is unclear that you may have overlooked.
- A resume should be a picture of you, so present yourself in the manner that you feel most comfortable with.
- Use good quality bond paper to print your resume on.
- Be sure to have a number of printed copies so they can be easily distributed during the interview.

Index